Fly and Spin Fishing for River Smallmouths

Fly and Spin Fishing

for River Smallmouths

Bruce Ingram

Ecopress

An Imprint of Finney Company

Lakeville, Minnesota

Ecopress
An Imprint of Finney Company
8075 215th Street West
Lakeville, Minnesota 55044
www.finneyco.com

ISBN 10: 1-893272-09-5
ISBN 13: 978-1-893272-09-5

Photography by Bruce Ingram.
Page 71 *Laptop and Telephone* © Luis Pedrosa.
Image from istockphoto.com.
Designed by Angela Wix
Edited by Lindsey Cunneen

Printed in the United States of America
1 3 5 7 9 10 8 6 4 2

Dedication

To my wife Elaine,
who patiently poses for my pictures and shows
how much she loves me in so many ways.

$\mathcal{C}$ontents

Part Four: *Fall Smallmouth Fishing*

Part Five: *Winter Smallmouth Fishing*

$\mathcal{I}$ntroduction

This is my fourth book, following *The James River Guide*, *The New River Guide*, and *The Shenandoah/Rappahannock Rivers Guide*. For this work, I wanted to give more detail to readers concerning how they can catch better quality river smallmouths, regardless of whether they fish with the long rod or spinning and baitcasting outfits. Plus, I wanted to cover how readers can enhance their on-water experience by camping and bird watching. But just as importantly, if not more so, I desired to give readers plenty of information on how they can protect the headwater springs and creeks in their home watersheds.

It's nice to read—and write—about how we can all catch more smallmouths, but if we are to have smallies to catch in the coming years, we sportsmen are going to have to pay more attention to what some biologists call our "watershed address." For what happens upstream from our home smallmouth rivers—those numerous springs, creeks, and mountain rills whose waters commingle to form America's upland rivers—is crucial to the future of river smallmouth fishing. I hope this book will give you some valuable information on how you can help protect the headwaters of your favorite smallmouth river, as well as give you some tidbits of wisdom to help you to become a more successful angler while afloat downstream.

$\mathcal{P}$reface: It's All Connected

A logical question might be why a section on wildlife habitat improvement and conservation easements appears at the beginning of a book largely about how to fly and spin fish for smallmouths on our nation's rivers. The blunt answer is that without protecting, improving, and creating wildlife habitat along our waterways, quality river smallmouth fishing will not exist in the future. I own land in Virginia and West Virginia and primarily fish and hunt in those two states with occasional forays into Tennessee and North Carolina. But regardless of where you live in this country, three main ways exist to improve and protect wildlife habitat.

The first is to work with state and national government agencies. Every state has its division of national resources—the folks in charge of managing game and nongame populations. Additionally, national government agencies such as the National Resources Conservation Service (which is part of the United States Department of Agriculture) have local offices across the country. Whenever I have had questions about my rural properties, the highly capable individuals from these state and national agencies have always been willing to visit my land and offer technical advice and assistance.

A second way is to place rural land that you own under conservation easements, or encourage rural landowners who you know to do so. The conservation easement movement began in earnest some 40 years ago and has since spread throughout the entire country. Conservation easements are where landowners agree to voluntarily give up certain developmental rights of their properties. The property protected and preserved forever, regardless of whether the landowner dies, moves, deeds the land to his children, or sells the land. In Part I, I tell how you can find out more about agencies that offer conservation easements in your state, as well as have a listing of other land conservation entities. Again, without exception, I have found the folks involved with easements extremely willing to help me protect my properties from development.

The third way is to support efforts of state and national governments to buy rural land. A state government can turn that land into a wildlife management area or park. The national government can add the property to its national forest holdings or other similar holdings. These public lands provide critical sanctuaries for wildlife and protect water quality, as well.

As an example of a watershed that would have benefited from conservation efforts such as these, I offer the Potomac and Shenandoah rivers in Virginia, West Virginia, and Maryland. At one time, these two rivers and their tributaries offered some of the best river smallmouth fishing in America. But now because of runoff from industrial poultry farms, cattle trampling and degrading stream banks, construction of homes and businesses in flood plains, and a host of other indignities, the fishing in these rivers has seriously degraded.

Instead of habitat destruction, imagine a river that has had native warm season grasses (such as switchgrass, Indian grass, and big bluestem) planted along its shores, where the farmer has fenced his cattle to keep them away from the river, where rural landowners have placed their lands under conservation easements (and not sold their lands to developers), and where state and national governments have bought properties and turned them into public lands.

Do anglers, hunters, bird watchers, nature photographers, and outdoor enthusiasts of all kinds need to know about ways to improve and protect wildlife habitat? The answer is an unqualified yes. Contact your local, state, and national government representatives to let them know that you support conservation efforts such as these. And also contact local and state land trust agencies and support their efforts.

Part One:

How to Protect Our Upland Rivers

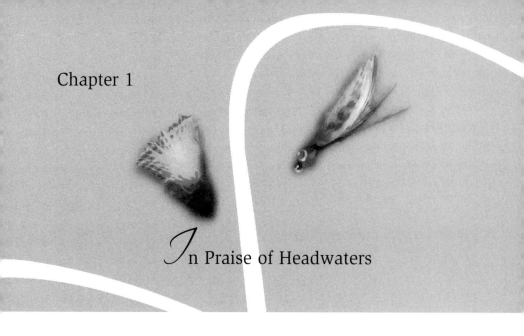

Chapter 1

In Praise of Headwaters

Sometimes when anglers become concerned about a river or lake fishery, they suggest various changes to length and creel regulations or perhaps request that catch and release or slot regulations be implemented. Sometimes, of course, the fisheries can benefit from those regulation changes.

But many times, the reason or cause for the "problem that needs fixing" originates not within the lake or river itself, but far upstream or up-lake in the headwaters. For here is a maxim that is often true about America's rivers and impoundments: If the headwaters and watershed are healthy, so is the main river or lake.

Bob Boeren, a forester for the Virginia Department of Forestry, explains why this is so.

"Absolutely, it matters to a lake or river that its headwaters are healthy," he said. "That's why two major goals of the department of forestry are to either maintain riparian forests or to restore/create them.

"A riparian zone [a buffer of trees, shrubs, and other vegetation between a stream and open ground] as narrow as 50 feet wide can completely remove excess nitrogen that is leaching from an agricultural or other area before that nitrogen reaches a stream. That zone can also filter sediment, phosphorus, and other forms of runoff."

If riparian zones exist around headwater springs and creeks, wildlife can benefit tremendously. Boeren adds that riparian zones: help stabilize stream banks, which prevents erosion; increase humidity, which benefits amphibians, snakes, and turtles; keep the water cooler, which benefits trout, minnows, and a host of other aquatic creatures;

and improve water quality, which benefits those that derive their water from these streams.

The riparian zones around headwater springs and creeks also benefit various other game and nongame species.

"One of the reasons that the forestry department likes to create riparian zones is so that we can connect wildlife corridors that were previously separated," continued Boeren. "A new riparian zone that connects two previous ones has obvious benefits for hunters and game animals. Deer and turkeys, for example, can now have travel ways between areas along these streams."

Nongame animals also benefit. A reforested headwater spring or stream can then host such songbirds as hooded warblers, Louisiana waterthrush, and common yellowthroats to name just a few. Later as the trees grow older, expect such songbirds as orchard orioles and parula warblers to appear. Boeren relates that riparian zones as narrow as 35 feet can offer significant advantages for wildlife and water quality.

"A good rule of thumb is to reforest that part of the stream that lies within the flood plain," he explained. "For a small stream, that might be anywhere from 35 to 100 or more feet. For a river, for example, the flood plain could be 300 to 500 feet or more, depending on the terrain."

State forest departments and other providers sell many varieties of trees that will thrive along headwaters. Boeren lists some possibilities: yellow poplars, sycamores, northern red oaks, black oaks, box elders, red maples, and dogwoods.

For landowners who want to log their property, tax credits exist for leaving a riparian zone intact. State forest departments also have riparian specialists that can assist landowners in creating buffers and protecting their headwaters.

From a Fisherman's Point of View

Scott Smith, a fisheries biologist for the Virginia Department of Game and Inland Fisheries (VDGIF), explains why headwater streams matter from a fisherman's viewpoint.

"Basically, water (and everything with and in it) goes downhill," he said. "Anything that happens in the watershed or headwaters will likely have some impact on larger rivers or reservoirs. A prime example is sedimentation. If you've got a lot of land-disturbing activities and poor riparian buffers upstream, that sediment will eventually end up in the bottom of rivers and lakes. Too much sediment is bad for just about all forms of aquatic life, from game fish on down to the things they feed on, on down to what the forage feeds on." Sediment covers spawning areas and stifles the growth of aquatic vegetation because less sunlight can filter through the water column.

Individuals Can Make a Difference

Just a few yards past the Roanoke County, Virginia, line on Route 785 lies the 289-acre Montgomery County farm of Ned and Janet Yost. The couple placed their property under a conservation easement with the Virginia Outdoors Foundation (VOF), in part because of their love and concern for streams, in this case, the headwaters of the North Fork of the Roanoke River.

"I am acutely conscious that how we treat the stream on our property impacts our neighbors downstream," said Ned Yost. "The area where we live is really a mini-divide. Catawba Creek, a headwater stream of the James River, starts on the other side of the county line, and so does the North Fork of the Roanoke, which flows in the opposite direction.

"I believe that at one time the North Fork likely contained native brook trout. One of my goals is to improve the habitat along my portion of the stream and perhaps convince my neighbors to do the same on their land. So that maybe one day, there can be a reproducing trout population in the stream."

Yost states that a conservation easement fit well with his long term goals for the property. The easement allows him to protect a historic site (McDonalds Mill, which was built in 1860), a forested mountainside (timbering, of course, is still allowed under the best management practices, as is hunting), and the property's traditional agricultural practices. Finally, he emphasizes that the need to protect headwaters transcends property lines and political boundaries such as county and state lines.

Not Just LIP Service

One of the most beneficial programs landowners can take advantage of is the Landowner Incentive Program (LIP) of the VDGIF, funded by a grant from the U.S. Fish and Wildlife Service and started in 2003. (*Note*: Many states feature similar programs.) Bill Bennett, a stream restoration biologist for the VDGIF, relates that the department is eager to work with landowners and that funds are available on a cost-share basis to achieve these objectives:

- Stop ongoing sedimentation, often by stabilizing weak or failing banks.

National Geographic has determined that this Highland County, Virginia, barn is the birthplace of both the James and Potomac rivers. The water falling off the left side begins the James and the right side, the Potomac. What the farmer who owns this barn does on his land matters downstream.

- Work with farmers to create livestock exclusion structures, such as fences, along streams.
- Install livestock watering systems that are positioned away from streams.
- Create or enhance riparian zones by planting trees and other vegetation.
- Re-engineer a stream so that its natural channel can be restored.

"The major goals of LIP are to protect, enhance, or improve habitats of endangered, threatened, or at-risk species such as the James spinymussel or the Roanoke logperch," says Bennett. "However, smallmouth bass, redbreast sunfish, and of course, many other game and nongame species will benefit from LIP, as well."

Personal Experience

In April of 2006, I bought 120 acres in the Sinking Creek Valley of Craig County, Virginia. The property lies at the literal continental divide

For More Information

○ Virginia Association of Soil and Water Conservation Districts: (804) 559-0324, www.vaswcd.org

○ Virginia Department of Conservation and Recreation: (804) 786-1712, www.dcr.virginia.gov

○ Virginia Department of Forestry: (434) 977-6555, www.dof.virginia.gov

○ For more information on riparian zones, click on the *Conserve* link. An excellent source for tree seedlings and various wildlife mixes is the Augusta Forestry Center in Crimora, Virginia, (540) 363-7000.

○ Virginia Department of Game and Inland Fisheries: (804) 367-1000, www.dgif.virginia.gov

○ Virginia Outdoors Foundation: www.virginiaoutdoorsfoundation.org

○ Virginia State Farm Services Agency: (804) 287-1503, www.fsa.usda.gov/va

○ Look under Conservation Reserve Enhancement Program (CREP). CREP is a voluntary program for agricultural landowners to receive payments and cost-share assistance to establish long term resource conserving cover.

○ National Resources Conservation Service: www.nrcs.usda.gov

○ U.S. Fish and Wildlife Service: www.fws.gov

○ Look for the Partners in Fish and Wildlife Program. USFWS personnel can put readers in touch with trained biologists in their home states.

Note: Similar agencies exist in all states and can be easily googled.

between the James and New rivers with the water running off one side of the mountain entering the watershed of the James and the water coursing down the other side flowing into the watershed of the New, specifically the headwater spring of Sinking Creek on my land.

After I purchased the land, I immediately contacted the Virginia Outdoors Foundation (VOF), and Tamara Vance, a deputy director for the VOF, came to tour the property with my wife Elaine and me. A major goal of ours was that the spring and creek be protected permanently, and Vance explained that a conservation easement is a marvelous way to accomplish that objective.

I already knew that such is the case because earlier I had placed our 272-acre tract on Potts Mountain in Craig County under a conservation easement with the VOF, making sure that a headwater spring of the James that lies between my property and that of a neighbor's would never be negatively impacted by any human activities.

My family lives on a 29-acre tract on Catawba Creek in Botetourt County, and we also own a 30-acre tract on Johns Creek in Craig County. Outside of time spent with my family, I experience no greater joy in life than hunting, fishing, and bird and wildlife watching while afield on these properties. My family wants to be good stewards of these special places.

Elaine says that I am "land and water crazy," and she's probably right. We even took a trip two years ago to view the Highland County, Virginia, barn that *National Geographic* confirmed as the literal beginning of the James and Potomac rivers with the barn roof "splitting the raindrops" between the two watersheds. What that Highland County farmer does on his land matters downstream, what I do on my properties matters downstream, and the same holds true for all Americans who own headwater springs and creeks.

Blueways: Rocking the Boat

Many communities have embraced greenways (trails along streams and through parks) and Rails to Trails (old railroad beds converted to hiking paths), but the concept of public blueways has been virtually unheard of. That is, until Scott Martin, director of Commerce & Leisure Services for Franklin County, Virginia, helped create blueways (officially designated float trips) on the Pigg and Blackwater rivers.

"The beauty of blueways is that by Franklin County authorizing stretches of the Pigg and Blackwater rivers as being noteworthy of this designation, people are more likely to want to experience these streams

A gathering of paddlers celebrating Franklin County, Virginia's blueways initiative before beginning a trip down the Blackwater River.

firsthand," said Martin. "And once people experience a natural resource, they often care more about its protection. I look at blueways as a win-win situation for the conservation of the two rivers and for attracting tourist dollars to the area."

Because the Pigg and Blackwater now have financial worth, politicians will now more likely want to protect them from potential environmental abuses, explains Martin. Another plus of blueways is that they are much cheaper to set up than, for example, hard surface trails. Martin relates that a community can purchase land and create a put-in and take-out for around $25,000, whereas, creating a mile of trail can cost as much as a million dollars.

In June 2005, I participated in the Breakfast on the Blackwater float, paddling this little-known river for the first time. Sycamores, box elders, and ironwood envelope the stream, and Acadian flycatchers, scarlet tanagers, and Eastern wood pee-wees were just a few of the numerous bird species that serenaded canoeists and kayakers. Part way through the float, participants stopped for a catered breakfast of pancakes, scrambled eggs, juice, and more.

For More Information

For more information on the annual Pigg River Ramble Canoe Race and Breakfast on the Blackwater float (held annually the first weekend in June) and blueways in general, visit www.historicrockymount.com. Readers can learn more about blueways in their home states by googling the name of their state and typing in *blueways* and/or *conservation efforts*.

Chapter 2

Conservation Easements:
Protecting the Future of Fly and Spin Fishing

As the real estate agent walked me around the Craig County, Virginia, property in April of 2006, I became more and more enthralled with it. At its highest point, the mountainous land borders the George Washington and Jefferson National Forest, and as we ambled up a hollow we successively spooked turkeys and deer. But my interest in the land skyrocketed when the agent showed me a spring bubbling from the forest floor.

"This is where Sinking Creek begins," the agent said. "If you buy this land, you'll not only own a headwater spring of the New River but also the first couple hundred yards of the creek."

"I'll buy it," I blurted out. Indeed, as soon as we returned to the agent's vehicle, I signed the contract. And a few weeks later after the contract had become final, I contacted the Virginia Outdoors Foundation (VOF) and began the process of placing the entire 120-acre property under a conservation easement. By January 2007 that process was finished, and I had ensured forever that the land would never be subdivided, that the property would always remain rural, and, very importantly, neither myself nor any future owner could ever conduct activities that could negatively impact the spring and creek on the property.

And by early May, the IRS sent me a refund check of $14,012 because of that easement. I received a financial reward just for doing my bit to protect wildlife habitat and the future of fishing on the New River Watershed. So what are conservation easements, how does an individual or group go about the process of instituting them, and why should readers consider them?

What Are Conservation Easements?

Conservation easements are voluntary and permanent deeded agreements that forever protect land from subdivisions and commercial development. An easement preserves certain values (such as scenic, agricultural, natural, and historical qualities of a landowner's property) while improving the owner's financial security through tax benefits and tax credit sales.

In fact, to be accepted, a proposed easement must preserve and protect in perpetuity the open-space values of the individual property. The values are described in the easement deed itself and in the documentation of the property that a land trust conducts.

Three times under the authority of the VOF, I have gone through the process of placing a conservation easement on various properties. This land trust follows a ten-step process, typical of what transpires in many states. The process can last anywhere from a few months to more than a year, but when an easement is finished, it is permanent and continues to exist for the property regardless of whether the initiator, any of his heirs, or anyone else owns it. Here is an abbreviated form of that process.

1: Consideration of Easement

After consulting with family members and perhaps tax and legal advisors, a landowner contacts a land trust (LT) to request information and to discuss general easement guidelines and possibilities. The LT and landowner discuss the stipulations in the easement that the landowner desires. The more restrictions on development that a landowner places, the greater the tax benefits are likely to be.

2: Site Visit

The LT and landowner look over the property, discussing long-term objectives and open-space values.

3: Preliminary Agreement

The landowner reaches a preliminary agreement with the LT on the proposed terms of the easement and property description. The landowner's lawyer and LT develop a draft easement for both parties to review.

4: Requirement for Title Opinion and Letter of Intent

The landowner provides a preliminary 20-year title report, usually prepared by an attorney. The landowner also submits a letter to the LT stating a desire to have an easement.

5: Staff Research
The LT completes research on the property, including matters of zoning classification, highway plans, and maps.

6: Board Approval
The LT board either accepts, rejects, or requests to modify the proposed easement.

7: Follow-up site visit
The LT makes a return visit for documentation of the property if necessary.

8: Baseline Documentation Report
The LT staff completes the file for the easement by obtaining documentation detailing the features of the property, such as boundaries and county tax maps. The landowner acknowledges the accuracy of this file.

9: Finalization Easement Draft
A lawyer sends the final easement, including the full legal property description, to the LT for review. The LT suggests edits, if any, and returns it to the attorney. If all goes well, the landowner then signs the easement.

10: Recordation
The LT records the easement in the local court. A copy of the recorded easement is sent to the landowner and/or his attorney.

Yes, this does sound complicated because, well, it is complicated and time consuming. But after a landowner has completed this process, she can be assured that her wishes for the future of the property will always have to be legally obeyed. After the legal process is complete, I have always contacted a certified assessor who then conducts a legal search to determine how much value the land has lost because it has been placed under a conservation easement. In our society, it is a fact of life that land that can be developed is worth more than land that cannot (although try telling that to a fly fisherman wading a pristine stream).

Because land under easement cannot be turned into a subdivision, strip mall, or parking lot, its value decreases. And since the landowner now owns property that has decreased in value, he can receive a tax refund, as I did, from the government. The legal process described above involving lawyers and assessors has always run me between $5,500 and $6,000, but I have always received grants from the VOF to pay those legal fees (separate from the $14,012 tax refund).

I want to emphasize that the landowner makes the decisions on what can and cannot be done to his property. For example, my 120-acre tract on

Conservation easements help protect the future of fishing and other outdoor recreational pursuits.

Sinking Creek can never be subdivided, nor can the 150-acre tract that I own on Potts Mountain. However, my 122-acre parcel adjacent to the 150-acre tract can be subdivided in half. On all these properties, I have had clauses inserted that protect the riparian zones and the scenic vistas of the ridge tops.

Easements: Why Fly and Spin Fishermen Should Know about Them

Roger Holnback, executive director of the Western Virginia Land Trust (WVLT), emphasizes that fly and spin fishermen should especially be interested in easements.

"Protecting headwater springs and streams is absolutely critical in assuring the future of fishing," Holnback told me. "Certainly one of the best ways to protect a headwater stream is to place a conservation easement on it. What's more, we're learning that when one landowner in a watershed protects his stream through an easement, others often want to do the same.

"For example, in Botetourt County [Virginia], a landowner, Ray Hundley, asked the WVLT to draw up an easement so that his headwater stream of the

James River would come under strict protection, which often means safeguarding a 100-foot-wide riparian zone on both sides of a stream. Then Hundley's downstream neighbor, Tom Kirlin, who is an avid fly fisherman, decided to do the same thing. The result is that now a long section of an important James River tributary has its riparian zone permanently protected. That can't help but be a good thing for anglers downstream."

Individual Goals

Even if a stream doesn't have much of a riparian zone, a conservation easement can help begin the process of restoring or creating a vibrant swath of native vegetation along a waterway.

"Land trust agents know the importance of a stream that is in unspoiled condition with wild trout or bass and aquatic insects," Holnback continued, "especially as compared to a stream that flows through a barren pasture with water characterized by high temperature and turbidity. We typically know who to contact at a state fisheries department who can help assist a landowner with stream improvement projects that create a vibrant riparian zone."

In the past year or so, I have talked with a number of Southwest Virginia landowners on how and why they have implemented conservation easements on their respective properties. Each of these individuals has different goals. For example, one Montgomery County landowner wanted to begin the process where he could one day angle for trout on his spring creek, which is part of the Roanoke River Watershed. So part of the foundation for this individual's conservation easement was placing restrictions on what type of activities could be done within the riparian zone, which the landowner wanted to protect permanently. He is now improving streamside habitat by planting native trees and warm season grasses. He sees the stream as a future haunt of bruiser browns.

Another landowner desired to restore a riparian zone that his dairy cattle had denuded, so he focused on erecting fencing that keeps the animals out of a headwater stream of the Roanoke River. Another individual, Jack Leffel, who is a dedicated smallmouth fan, owns land that borders the James River. Leffel placed an easement on his riverfront property and is now working to restore the riparian zone so that the smallmouths will have more places to hold. A fourth landowner, Paul Hinlicky of Roanoke County, has purchased 60 acres as a fixer-upper project, with goals of protecting spring seeps that drain into a James tributary and planting native warm season grasses that draw game animals.

On my three properties under easements, I have protected headwater springs and streams in both the James and New River Watersheds, improved wildlife habitat, and made money through timber sales (from judicial timber cutting). Fishing, hunting, farming, and logging remain "values" under conservation easements and, thus, are allowed.

You Too Can Make A Difference

For the past 25 years, I have held two full-time jobs as a high school English teacher and outdoor writer. During that time, I have sold over 1,800 magazine articles and written four books. With that writing income, I have bought 486 acres of rural land and have placed 392 of those acres under conservation easements. With those easements, in a small but important way, I have done my part to protect our outdoor heritage and its future.

You can do the same. Fishermen are typically well educated and financially secure. Many of you have the potential ability (through personal income or fishing clubs and organizations you belong to) to place headwater springs, streams, and portions of trout and bass waterways under conservation easements. Please consider doing so on either land you own or that your club owns or leases. You might also want to consider contacting rural landowners on whose property you fly or spin fish. Remember, you'll be doing a service to not only current day outdoorsmen but also to those who follow us in the decades and centuries to come.

Land Trusts: A National Movement

Although my experience with conservation easements has just been in Virginia, readers should understand that land trusts are a national phenomenon.

"All 50 states have enabling legislation that allows land trusts and conservation easements," said Roger Holnback. "Sometimes, the trusts are state wide entities; sometimes they cover one region or one county or even just one valley. More and more, citizens are starting land trusts if they see a need for them in their particular locales."

Here are some examples:

- The Lancaster Farmland Trust has solely worked to preserve farmland in Lancaster County, Pennsylvania.
- Part of the mission of the San Diego Land Conservancy is to preserve the remaining farms in that area of California.
- Connecticut features three statewide land trusts and 109 local ones.
- The Blue Ridge Rural Land Trust, a regional group, focuses only on protecting land in northwestern North Carolina.

To locate land trusts in your home state, google it by typing in your state's name and the words land trust. The Land Trust Alliance Web site (listed above) also offers links to trusts in every state.

Tax Breaks

Holnback says that nationwide, the federal government and IRS recognize that the individual property owner who places his land under a conservation easement is giving up development potential (that is, losing money) and therefore deserves a tax break or refund of some sort.

As noted earlier, I received a refund check of $14,012 from the IRS on land that I bought for $165,000. Next year, I am slated to receive another refund. The exact amount will depend on a host of factors, such as how much money I earn from my other job and how many years I want the refunds spread over.

Everyone's tax situation is different and that is why I pay a tax consultant to help me. State and local tax benefits commonly exist as well throughout the country. But, frankly, many people who love the land (myself included) would have done a conservation easement even if there were no tax breaks.

For More Information

National Land Conservation Organizations
   American Farmland Trust: www.farmland.org
   Land Trust Alliance: www.lta.org
   National Trust for Historic Preservation: www.nationaltrust.org
   The Conservation Fund: www.conservationfund.org
   Trust for Public Land: www.tpl.org

State Resources
   Many states have local and state-wide land trust organizations. For example, in the Old Dominion, the Virginia Outdoors Foundation (www.virginiaoutdoorsfoundation.org) is the umbrella group for dozens of regional land trusts around the Commonwealth. I belong and donate money to two regional land trusts that operate where I live in Southwest Virginia: the New River Land Trust (www.newriverlandtrust.org) and the Western Virginia Land Trust (www.westernvirginialandtrust.org).

Chapter 3

Minnows and Mussels: What They Can Teach Us

"Ah, there he is, that's a very good sign," exulted Nathaniel "Than" Hitt, a graduate student in the Department of Fisheries and Wildlife Sciences at Virginia Tech.

The scene behind our house on Catawba Creek in Botetourt County, Virginia, was a little surreal. Wearing a 35-pound electroshocking "backpack," Hitt was wielding what looks like a long hoe with a circular metal object on the end of it, but it was really a device that sends an electric current into a localized section of the creek. Behind Hitt, my son Mark stood ready with a net to scoop up any dazed denizens that float to the surface. Once Mark corralled a critter, he deposits it into an aerated white bucket on the stream bank where later Hitt would identify and number the species before releasing it.

The *he* that Hitt was so excited to capture is a longfin darter (*Etheostoma longimanum*), an indicator species for the upper James River basin—for the health of bass populations as well as the health of the entire river ecosystem. Simply stated, if the stream conditions are such that this darter exists in good numbers, chances are that smallmouth bass, for example, are also present in good numbers. Conversely, if habitat conditions deteriorate and the longfin darter starts to disappear, the odds are that the fishing will soon become worse as game fish will no longer be able to reproduce and survive in sufficient numbers.

"In the upper James River Basin, species such as the longfin darter, mountain redbelly dace, and longnose dace serve as an early warning system," explained Hitt, as he released the longfin back into the creek. "For example, some fish species require clean gravels for spawning and cannot tolerate sedimentation. When those species disappear, that could forecast declines in species that are somewhat more tolerant of sediment, such as smallmouth bass. Even the smallest minnows, darters, suckers, and sculpins can tell us something important about the quality of our streams, if we know how to listen."

A new program of the Virginia Department of Environmental Quality (VDEQ) aims to help with that listening. The VDEQ's Probabilistic Monitoring Program (called ProbMon) was initiated in 2001 to assess the status of the Commonwealth's streams and rivers using invertebrates found in the stream. Currently, Hitt is working with his advisor, Dr. Paul Angermeier, to incorporate stream fishes into the ProbMon program as a pilot project.

"Stream fishes provide new insight about environmental quality because they have unique habitat requirements," Hitt explained. "And because some species can move long distances, they may help us better understand the status of entire watersheds."

In Search of the James Spinymussel

Several weeks later, I was standing in Johns Creek, a Craig County tributary of Craig Creek, which in turn flows into the James River. Johns is typical of many tributaries of the James in Western Virginia; it features

If you want to catch river smallmouths like this one, you need to understand what minnows and mussels mean to fishermen.

New Program Available For Landowners

One of the best things landowners along waterways can do to improve stream habitat for game and nongame species is to become involved in the Landowner Incentive Program (LIP), according to Louise Finger, a VDGIF stream restoration biologist.

"The VDGIF administers the federally-funded LIP that provides 75 percent cost share on a voluntary basis to private landowners for protection and/or restoration of streams in target watersheds that contain threatened, endangered, or at-risk aquatic species. The goal of this program is to protect, restore, or enhance habitat for rare, aquatic species," Finger said.

"Within these watersheds, protecting headwater streams is of the highest importance," Finger continued. "LIP practices employed to protect and enhance water quality and aquatic habitat include livestock fencing, alternative watering source development, riparian buffer planting, bank stabilization, and stream restoration. These practices reduce bank erosion, stream sedimentation, and nutrients in runoff. They also improve wildlife habitat in the riparian corridor and aquatic habitat within the stream channel itself by providing cover, shade, and food."

The Watersheds and Some of the Species Targeted for Protection:

○ Upper Tennessee Drainage:
31 species of endangered mussels, yellowfin madtom

○ Lower New River:
candy darter, hellbender

○ Upper Roanoke River:
Roanoke logperch, orangefin madtom, Atlantic pigtoe

○ Upper James River and Rivanna River:
James spinymussel, Atlantic pigtoe

Three VDGIF Stream Restoration Biologists work directly with landowners to identify and implement the practices appropriate to each site. These biologists are based out of the Verona, Forest, and Marion offices.

○ Louise Finger, of Verona:
(540) 248-9377, louise.finger@dgif.virginia.gov

○ Bill Bennett, of Forest:
(434) 525-7522, ext. 113, bill.bennett@dgif.virginia.gov

○ Justin Laughlin, of Marion:
(276) 783-4860, justin.laughlin@dgif.virginia.gov

Note: Across the country, state fishery departments employ stream restoration biologists. Contact the biologist in your home state for more information.

trout in its headwaters, and smallmouth bass, rock bass, redbreast sunfish, and fall fish throughout most of its length. Next to me were Brian Watson, a wildlife diversity biologist, and Melanie Stine, assistant biologist, both from the Virginia Department of Game and Inland Fisheries' (VDGIF) regional office in Forest. We were searching for a specific species of mussel that might live in a section of creek that borders land I own.

"Johns Creek is a high priority area for the VDGIF Landowner Incentive Program (see below) since it has the best-known population of the endangered James spinymussel," Brian said. "Mussels are excellent indicators of water quality, because as filter feeders they process what is in the water. Just like the canary in a coal mine, they can be the first indicator of a potential water quality problem. If the James spinymussel starts to disappear, we could see a decline in the trout population and that disappearance could eventually be seen in other fish populations like smallmouth and sunfish, as well.

"Water quality and habitat degradation are the primary reasons for the decline of freshwater mussels. It is not uncommon for anglers to comment that mussels used to be more prevalent in streams where there has been a decline in fishing quality. There is a link here and the mussels are trying to tell us there is a problem—we only need to listen. The spinymussel is typically more sensitive to water quality changes and habitat alterations than other mussel species so their decline should be an early warning signal."

I was confident that we would find the spinymussel in the stretch of creek that runs through my land. I had fished this section of Johns Creek since 1970 and owned it since 1983. But as Brian positioned his green "view bucket" with its plexi-glass bottom on the creek's surface so that he can scan the bottom and Melanie donned snorkeling gear so that she can creep along the substrate, I found myself passionately hoping that they will locate a spinymussel, just as many times I have fished the stream passionately hoping to catch smallmouths.

My land is not just a place for me to fish and hunt on, but a place for me to be a good steward. How I treat this little postage stamp of property matters to all those who live downstream.

Brian and Melanie searched for several hours but could not locate a single James spinymussel. They did encounter shells of the Eastern elliptio (the most common mussel on the Atlantic slope), Atlantic pigtoe (state threatened and relatively rare throughout Virginia), and that ubiquitous invader, the Asian clam. Brian could tell I was dispirited.

"Sometimes it can take four or five trips to a stream section before we can find a spinymussel," he consoled. "Your riparian buffer and water quality look good. On the other hand, your stream habitat of bedrock and cobble is not conducive to finding a spinymussel. It typically thrives in flowing areas with stable pebble, sand, and gravel, which are lacking on your property."

"However, you should know that your healthy riparian buffer is a plus for the James spinymussel and game fish downstream," he added.

Like a trout fisherman who has a honey hole he can always count on, Brian then proclaimed that he could drive us to a place upstream that was "guaranteed" to contain spinymussels.

"Recently, we found over 80 there in a little 20-yard stretch," he exclaimed.

Two minutes after arriving, Brian corrals a creeper, a species relatively uncommon in the James Watershed. But a minute or so later, Melanie surfaced, displaying a wide grin. In her hand was a James spinymussel.

I was as excited as if I had just caught a four-pound smallmouth from the James, and I took pictures of the creature. Then Melanie carefully returned the spinymussel to the same place she found it, just as I would have released a smallmouth. The fates of the two species are related, and minnows and mussels do mean more to anglers than many people realize.

Indicator Fish Species In Virginia

"Stream fishes can provide a wealth of information about environmental quality and sport fishing opportunities," said Than Hitt. "Although quite diverse in their appearance and behavior, several stream fishes share strict requirements for high-quality habitats. As a result, these species indicate environmental quality and provide an early warning system to avoid future sport fish declines."

The following are examples of freshwater indicator fishes from the major basins in the Old Dominion, Tennessee, North Carolina, West Virginia, and Maryland. Look for these fishes as good signs of environmental quality and sport fishing in your watershed. For pictures of these fishes, visit www.cnr.vt.edu/efish.

James River Basin
Longfin darter (*Etheostoma longimanum*)
Torrent sucker (*Thoburnia rhothoeca*)

New River Basin
Candy darter (*Etheostoma osburni*)
Tonguetied minnow (*Exoglossum laurae*)

Potomac River Basin
Northern hogsucker (*Hypentelium nigricans*)
Slimy sculpin (*Cottus cognatus*)

Roanoke River Basin
Orangefin madtom (*Noturus gilberti*)
Roanoke logperch (*Percina rex*)

Tennessee River Basin
Blotched chub (*Erimystax insignis*)
Gilt darter (*Percina evides*)

Chapter 4

*W*orking Together to Improve Wildlife Habitat

As dawn began to break across the Franklin County, Virginia, cut corn field, I tuned into the various sounds of an early November morning while resting my muzzleloader across my knees. Sitting under the low hanging limbs of an ancient red cedar tree in the middle of the field, I soon heard the yelps of jakes and jennies coming from the heavily wooded riparian zone below. From the overgrown fence row to my right, I harked to the whistled call notes of a bobwhite covey.

Behind me in a woodlot, I detected the lilting notes of song sparrows, Carolina wrens, rufous-sided towhees, followed by the tinkling sounds of a ruby crowned kinglet that flew into the cedar. Shortly afterward, I espied a mature doe enter the field from the woods where the turkeys roosted. I slowly mounted the smoke pole, trained the scope on the doe's vitals, clicked off the safety, and fired. Seconds later, I was standing over the doe, preparing to field dress her.

I was afield on the 1,000-acre farm of Johnny and Sharon Angell of Penhook—two of the most dedicated stewards of wildlife habitat that I have ever had the pleasure to meet. Many of the management projects that take place on this Franklin County farm are done for the benefit of wildlife. These include the undisturbed riparian zones along the Pigg River and its tributaries, the overgrown fence rows, the corn and soybeans fields that Sharon periodically bush hogs for wildlife, the warm season grasses that the Angells plant, their planned elimination of cold season grasses such as fescue, and the prescribed burns that the couple conducts. Fescue, a popular choice for a trim beautiful lawn, is sterile and indigestible by many animals; like most cold season grasses, it has limited nutritional or cover value.

"I consider myself a redneck environmentalist," laughed Johnny as I talked with him and Sharon in their farmhouse. "When I was younger, I was always trying to see how much my land could produce. But as I've matured, I've come to realize the importance of land for the future of wildlife. And I've come to really enjoy providing and creating quality habitat for game and nongame wildlife. Sharon's and my ultimate goal is to have a place where the wildlife can continue on after us."

Besides the activities already mentioned, Johnny and Sharon have a host of other ongoing projects. Within the past two years, they have learned that rearing prawns, often called freshwater shrimp, is a land-friendly activity that also offers the potential for steady income. The couple also grows loblolly pines for timber and has found that quail take to these stands for their first seven to eight years.

Johnny is fond of saying that "one way to get a big tree is to start with a little one," and toward that end the couple has planted fast-maturing sawtooth oaks. The twosome also tries to leave mature oaks as shelter trees whenever they perform a strategic cut. And every year Sharon proclaims that she "wears out a bush hog" in an effort to keep fields planted with warm season grasses from being overrun with saplings and other vegetation.

Virginia Department of Game and Inland Fisheries (VDGIF) biologist Marc Puckett helped the Angells draw up a habitat improvement plan. He offered these tips.

"As far as the warm season grasses are concerned, they are certainly better for wildlife than fescue," said Puckett. "A mixture of Indian grass, Blackwell switchgrass, and big bluestem at a rate of two pounds per acre each is a good wildlife mixture. If your goal is primary forage, plant them at a rate of three pounds each."

The biologist suggests that landowners sow these warm season grasses in late May to early June. The best method of establishment is to hay the existing grass in late April or early May. Once the grass renews itself about six inches, spray with two quarts per acre of Roundup. Let the plot die back a week or two, then no-till plant into the killed grass.

Puckett emphasizes three objectives: create a firm seedbed, do not plant the seeds more than ¼-inch deep, and manage weed competition. Also, landowners should attempt to plant when the ground is not wet or soft, especially when dealing with heavy or clay soils. Adding a legume such as partridge pea to the grass mix is also helpful. Finally, disturbing the soil (such as disking) every three years is a good strategy, too.

Sharon Angell, shown here examining a food plot, and her husband Johnny strive to have a wildlife-friendly farm.

Crop Field Edges

Mark Puckett proclaims that crop field edges are some of the best places for landowners to create wildlife habitat.

"Many landowners are not very crazy about just letting weeds grow," he said. "However, native vegetation is what quail, for example, need. One of the simplest and most effective techniques for establishing a field border is leaving an unplanted edge a minimum of 25 feet out from the woods edge. In this area, native grasses and weeds will grow. Nesting quail and turkeys and their poults will use these areas."

Puckett adds that these areas can be maintained by disking ⅓ of the total field border acreage every year during late February or March. Most crop field edges, particularly those along wooded areas, are poor crop producers. Competition from trees for nutrients and sunlight often make these edges net losses for the farmer.

"From farmers' standpoints, I'm not sure why they would waste time, seed, and chemicals in these areas, particularly when cost share exists to help farmers leave these acres for wildlife," continued the biologist.

Puckett gives simple hints for planting a field crop edge:

- Northern edges are best because they receive the most sunlight.
- Use the tree species that grow tallest nearest the woods and progress outwardly with lower growing shrubs and plants.
- A good progression from inside out would be sawtooth oaks (can produce acorns in five to ten years), wild plums (great for sandy soils), VA-70 lespedeza (good for a variety of soils), and a mixture of Korean, kobe, and partridge pea (five, five, and two pounds, per acre respectively).
- Sow the mixture in late February or early March, although it will do satisfactorily up to mid-April. These species do well on clay and sandy loam but not as well on very sandy soil.
- Don't worry about native weeds springing up. They are a bonus for wildlife.
- Lespedezas and partridge peas are annuals, but they reseed heavily. Light disking in February and March will help them reseed.

Puckett concludes by emphasizing that quail chicks, turkey poults, and a host of songbird species will utilize these crop edges for they are somewhat closed at the canopy level, thus serving as protection from overhead predators. But these plants allow easy mobility underneath, as well as hosting numerous insects (which are critical food for young birds) such as beetles, leafhoppers, and grasshoppers.

Creating My Own Wildlife Oasis

In April 2006, Bill Moss of the National Resources Conservation Service (which is part of the U.S. Department of Agriculture) visited land I own in Craig County. Our mission was to begin the process of establishing a warm season grasses meadow of Indian grass, Blackwell switchgrass, and big bluestem. The summer before, a logger had created an 11-acre clear-cut to create habitat diversity. The meadow would bring additional diversity to my mostly wooded property.

Moss began the process by taking a soil test, which determined, as is true across much of the Southeast, that the soil needed lime. Then he conducted a GPS reading to delineate the one-acre section that had been designated as future grassland. The reading also helped determine exactly how much lime and seed would be needed, as well as enabling Moss to "map it," that is, have an aerial photograph of the precise spot.

"The reason for mapping the field is to measure the acreage for treatment, identify the field on a map and on the landowner's conservation plan," he said.

Finally, Moss listed the typical steps along the way for a warm season grasses meadow to come into existence:

- Create a seedbed, clear stumps, rocks, and woody debris.
- Moss recommends a "carrier" so that the "fluffy" seed is not blown way. A good choice is a fertilizer with very low nitrogen content such as 5-10-10 or less. Mix about half fertilizer and half seed to broadcast. Plant from May 15 to July 1.
- Broadcast seed (two parts switchgrass to one part Kaw big bluestem to one part Cheyenne Indian grass; also add a legume like two parts partridge pea) after lightly disking the area.
- Afterward, at least half the seed should be visible.
- Drag soil to cover seed. Then pray for a lot of rain.
- A firebreak of an annual or perennial could be planted around the meadow.
- For additional habitat diversity, consider setting aside land in the middle of the meadow as a perennial or annual food plot.
- Expect two years to pass before the meadow becomes well-established.
- When weed competition occurs, open the canopy to sunlight by setting a mower at least 12 inches high to clip the tops of weeds without cutting emerging grass.
- Consider applying for cost share through WHIP (Wildlife Habitat Incentive Program), which can pay up to 75 percent of the cost. The sign up period is October 1 through January 13.

VDGIF wildlife biologist Betsy Stinson recommends that landowners have in mind the answers to these questions before starting a project.

- What is the total acreage of the property and how much acreage will be managed?
- Is the acreage to be managed as forested or open land?
- What are your management goals?
- What species are you interested in managing for?
- How active are you willing to be in your management? That is, how much time do you have to manage the property, and do you have access to tractor and disk, and/or bush hog? Knowing what type of time commitment you are able to make in managing your wildlife area helps biologists develop a wildlife habitat plan that is best suited to your needs.

Stinson also recommends that property owners obtain a topo map that delineates the property boundaries and the areas that they are interested in managing. Also, an aerial photo of your property is useful to have before starting on your wildlife management plan.

For More Information

○ National Resources Conservation Service: www.nrcs.usda.gov

○ The NRCS administers WHIP, as well as programs designed to curb water erosion and wind damage, conserve soil and water resources, stabilize streams, manage manure, grasslands, and forest lands, and establish wildlife habitat. *Note:* This is a national agency. The agencies below have counterparts in every state.

○ Virginia Association of Soil and Water Conservation Districts: (804) 559-0324, www.vaswcd.org

○ Virginia Department of Forestry: (434) 977-6555, www.dof.virginia.gov

○ An excellent source for tree seedlings and various wildlife mixes is the Augusta Forestry Center in Crimora: (540) 363-7000

○ Virginia Department of Game and Inland Fisheries: (804) 367-1000, www.dgif.virginia.gov

○ For information on seed and plant providers, VDGIF biologist Betsy Stinson recommends this site: www.dgif.virginia.gov/wildlife/plantdealers/index.asp

Chapter 5

Learning New Ways:
Ray Hundley, Veteran Sportsman and Farmer

As someone who has put 392 acres of Craig County, Virginia, land under a conservation easement, I always like to call other people who live near my Botetourt County home and have likewise placed their properties under an easement. And so it was that I contacted Ray Hundley and his wife Faye who live outside of Gala.

When I did so, I received an invitation from 79-year-old Ray to visit the couple's 800-acre farm. Before going, I called Roger Holnback, executive director of the Western Virginia Land Trust, to learn more about the particulars of the Hundley's easement. The couple has placed a riparian easement on 32 acres of streamside habitat along 2.6 miles of Sinking Creek and one of its tributaries.

"Ray and Faye Hundley have been good stewards of their land since they bought it back in the early 1950s," Holnback told me. "Sinking Creek is a beautiful, clear, cold water stream—shaded by overhanging native trees and full of native wildlife—that feeds into the James River. Just the type of stream that we are trying to preserve in order to protect Virginia's water supply at its sources.

"Ray told me that if he ever sees mud in the water, he heads upstream weather permitting to find out what caused it, whether the cause is natural or man-made. If all those who own river and creek frontage cared for their streams like the Hundleys do, we wouldn't have nearly the water quality and quantity problems we have. So those of you who use water on down the James, including Richmond, can thank the Hundleys for helping to protect your water supply."

When I arrived at the Hundley's farmhouse, the couple invited me to sit at their kitchen table. Once there, they peppered me with questions concerning current conservation topics of interest: had I heard about the rediscovery of the ivory-billed woodpecker, why were whip-poor-will numbers down, what did I know about mountaintop mining? Then I asked why they had placed a conservation easement on their property.

"To save the land for the future, for our grandkids, or whoever owns the land in the future," Faye told me. "To protect this little part of nature forever."

Ray agreed.

"I've always been a hunter and interested in wildlife," he said. "It's so important for the future of hunting and wildlife to protect habitat. Another thing is that I thought when water got to costing more than gasoline, it was time to start protecting the water. That's a major reason why we put an easement on the land-protecting our creeks."

Faye then added that water would be the most precious commodity to the people of the twenty-first century, comparing its importance to petroleum, which she believes was the most important commodity of the previous 100 years. Ray then praised the work of the WVLT.

"Roger Holnback was so helpful to us and answered all our questions," said Ray. "He walked over the land with us and told us how we could protect the creeks. A landowner isn't alone when he places an easement on his property. He has somebody like Roger to answer questions and help monitor things. That was an assurance to Faye and me. And it was an assurance to us

Faye and Ray Hundley are true stewards of their land and can serve as models for other landowners.

that we were doing something good for future generations. Of course, it doesn't hurt that conservation easements can reduce the taxes on your land."

Many landowners mistakenly believe that they cannot continue to conduct normal management practices on their properties if they place easements on them. Such is not the case. For example, Hundley recently wanted to create some habitat diversity in the forested part of his farm by doing some logging, plus earn some money from the cutting. To that end, he clear-cut three eight-acre blocks, each of which followed the natural contour of the land. And none of which came within 200 feet of the easement-protected streams.

DMAP for Better Deer Hunting

Just as the Hundleys have lately placed a conservation easement on their land, they have become recent fans of the Virginia Game Department's Deer Management Assistance Program (DMAP) initiative.

"I've always been interested in deer hunting and management," said Ray. "I wanted to improve the quality of the deer here, not just create bigger bucks. So I contacted the game department. Biologist Jay Jeffries came over, examined the land, and recommended that our goal be to kill more does and fewer bucks.

"That wasn't a hard thing for me to do. But I have to admit that, at first, it was hard for some of the people that hunt on the place. Back when I started deer hunting in the 1940s, we killed whatever the law said we could kill—which meant mostly bucks of whatever size or age. But times have changed, and many places, including my own, have too many does. The old way of thinking that killing a buck is always better than killing a doe is no good now."

Ever since DMAP has been in place on his land, Ray says that more does than bucks have been harvested each year. And the animals being killed are weighing an average of ten pounds more than previously harvested whitetails. Readers should understand that hunting is a very important way to keep wildlife numbers, especially deer, in balance with the land. If there are too many deer, over-browsing occurs and that is bad for the health of the deer herd as well as other game and nongame animals that have now lost critical food and cover sources.

Deer and Turkey Hunting Wisdom

Spend any time around Ray Hundley, and conversation will inevitably turn to deer and turkey hunting. I asked him to share his favorite tips, based on his experience as a hunter for over 60 years.

- "For deer, the most important thing is that you [have] to be there, you can't kill a deer sitting in the house," laughed Ray. "I will go before daylight and hunt until around one o'clock, and then come back out around three o'clock and hunt until dark. Most of the big bucks I have killed have been between 9 and 11 a.m."

- "For big bucks, always hunt the ridges in the mornings," he said. "That's always true, except during the rut when the bucks can be anywhere."

- "If you want to kill a mature gobbler, don't call so much, which is what too many people do," said Ray. "If he hears you, he knows where you are. Make that gobbler come hunting for you, instead of the other way around."

- "If a gobbler seems to be more interested in his hens than he is in your calls, make him want to fight," said Hundley. "Make some fighting purrs and start a commotion."

The DGIF's Deer Management Assistance Program (DMAP)

Matt Knox, the game's department individual most responsible for keeping tabs on Virginia's deer herd, is a huge booster of DMAP.

"DMAP is probably our most popular deer management program," he said. "Most people think if it as QDM (Quality Deer Management), because 85 percent of our DMAP cooperators (covering 1.2 million acres) practice some form of QDM. But DMAP is much more versatile than that.

"The secret to me is that DMAP has no stated objective, it is an open-ended deer management program, which we tailor to meet the objective of the landowner [or] club. Also, because they are all required to collect data from every deer they kill, DMAP cooperators and the hunters that hunt on these properties become much more knowledgeable about deer biology and management. It is a win-win situation for the department."

For More Information

- ○ Virginia Outdoors Foundation:
  www.virginiaoutdoorsfoundation.org
- ○ Western Virginia Land Trust:
  www.westernvirginialandtrust.org
- ○ New River Land Trust:
  www.newriverlandtrust.org
- ○ Valley Conservation Council:
  www.valleyconservation.org

Note: Similar organizations exist in every state.

Chapter 6

Living Easy on the Land

Not too many years after Jack Spigle took over Penn Farm in 1967 from his father-in-law, he began to have doubts about how the Botetourt County cattle farm on the James River was being run. Spigle had always been a hunter, fisherman, and conservationist, and he cared deeply about wildlife.

"I could see the negative impact that my cattle operations had both on the streams that flowed through my land and the James River," said Spigle. "And I also knew that what was happening on my land ultimately had a negative impact on the Chesapeake Bay. The cattle were lounging in my three creeks and degrading the stream banks. And the bottomland on my property didn't have any quail—much of the vegetation was gone. It was very obvious to me that where you have cattle, you don't have quail.

"I have been a quail hunter my entire adult life, and I grew up on a farm where my brother and I had to take care of the cattle. So I badly wanted to implement practices on Penn Farm that would be good both for cattle and for quail and other wildlife."

The information that Spigle needed in order to accomplish those twin goals was found at such organizations as the Farm Service Agency (FSA), Natural Resources Conservation Service (NRCS), Virginia Cooperative Extension (VCE), Mountain Castles Soil & Water Conservation District (MCSWCD), Department of Conservation and Recreation (DCR), and the Virginia Department of Game and Inland Fisheries (VDGIF).

What's more, farmers and landowners often do not have to bear the full cost of implementing practices that are beneficial for their land and for wildlife. The Virginia Agricultural Best Management Practice (BMP) offers 75 percent cost share and a 25 percent tax credit. Tax credits are also available on eligible voluntary conservation practices subject to prior approval. What this means is that a government agency will pay 75 percent of the total cost on projects, for example, that reduce sediment, erosion, or nutrients entering streams. Then the landowner will receive a 25 percent tax credit for the rest of the price. If, for example, a project cost $1000, the landowner would receive $750 (or 75 percent) and then on the remaining $250, the landowner would receive $62.50 (which is 25 percent of $250). As Spigle noted, "Farmers are tax payers and they should take advantage of these services. These organizations have great people working for them, and they are available to give technical assistance."

For example, one of the practices that Jack Spigle implemented was to fence all his streams and woods, thus excluding cattle from those areas. For the former, besides reducing erosion and the amount of pollution entering the streams, he created valuable riparian habitat (Spigle also has planted trees along the fenced-in streams). By fencing the farm's woodlots, the Botetourt County landowner was able to make his land more hospitable to deer, turkeys, and numerous game and nongame species. Cattle can do great damage to vegetation and the forest floor if allowed to roam through woodlots.

Another practice that Spigle implemented was rotational grazing of paddocks, which improves soil and plants and results in better animal growth and performance. A *paddock* is an enclosure within an overall fenced area. For example, Jack will often have his cattle confined to one paddock while two nearby paddocks regenerate.

In July 2005, I visited Spigle at Penn Farm. He first took me to one of his frost-proof water tanks. Water runs from a well through pipes to the tank, and cattle press on a ball on top of the tanks. When the ball lowers, the bovines can then drink. As impressive as this system is, what I found to be truly ingenious is how the water tanks dot Penn Farm. For example, Spigle has placed tanks where two or three paddocks intersect. That way, he doesn't need as many tanks or pipelines—or the expense of constructing them.

Another aspect of the farm that Spigle is justifiably proud of is his song bird population. When I got out of my car, barn swallows immediately flew over me and several mourning doves flushed. After we left the water tank, Jack had to make a stop to check one of his bluebird nesting boxes. All in all, I probably heard or saw some 20 avian species during the two hours I toured the farm—not bad for a hot July day.

Jack Spigle, shown here with his cattle, has created a network of paddocks around his farm that allows fields to rest and regenerate—thus protecting the land from being overgrazed.

Our next stop was at one of the regenerating paddocks. In some places, the vegetation was several feet high while on the other side of the enclosure, cows were contentedly consuming grass. Jack told me that he had no set time for when he would move his cattle from the paddock they were in. Such factors as rain, vegetation growth, and number of cattle all affect how long livestock will take to munch the grass down to a level that makes it necessary for them to be removed to another paddock.

How Landowners Can Help Make Land More Hospitable for Quail and Other Wildlife

VDGIF biologist Marc Puckett emphasizes that farmers are not the enemy of wildlife and that cattle and quail can go together with the proper adjustments. He noted, "My number one concern is the preservation of the family farm and the farming way of life. When we start to lose farms to other uses, we lose wildlife, as well."

○ Obtain aerial photo of property. This helps when looking for opportunities to help wildlife and to develop a plan or goal.

○ Decide whether you want more or less of a specific game or nongame species.

○ Obtain publications on topics such as warm season grasses, food plots, and wildlife needs. Examples are *Beyond the Food Patch: A Guide to Providing Quail Habitat* and *Successful Wildlife Plantings*. Check the VDGIF's Web site for more information.

○ For wildlife and especially for quail, position fences creatively. For example, a fence placed 25 to 30 feet from a woodlot will allow a variety of plants to flourish. Landowners also could plant lespedeza in this area and spray to kill fescue.

○ Work with existing native plants.

○ Fenced out areas along streams are good places to plant partridge peas and lespedeza, for example.

○ Plant native warm season grasses such as switchgrass, Indian grass, and big bluestem; these grasses provide nutritional food and quality cover to wildlife. Bottomlands are good places to establish these plants.

○ Perennial food plots are better than annual ones. Cost is lower, and the soil does not have to be tilled as often, so there is less erosion and fewer nutrients lost.

As an angler and a fan of the James River, I was highly impressed with what Spigle is doing to improve water quality. At Penn Farm, thanks to the fences that run parallel to all sides of the three creeks and along the bank of the James, the water flows clean and clear past heavily forested and vegetated shorelines. Once, Jack stopped to show me a deer track along one of his streams. The water was cool to the touch; pickerel frogs leaped into the water, and minnows darted away.

Jack Spigle has a passion for quail and bird hunting, and that fervor shows in one of his current projects.

"I am trying to eliminate fescue from areas of my farm," he told me. "Quail chicks just can't survive in fescue. The stuff is so thick that they can't make their way through it. Quail need fairly open ground with a canopy overhead."

With his desire to improve the bobwhite population, as well as benefit other wildlife, Spigle is planting such things as switchgrass, partridge pea, and clover. He also regularly conducts controlled burns; typically a parcel is burned every three years. Right after a controlled burn, wildlife—deer, turkeys, field sparrows, meadowlarks, and more—will congregate. Later, early successional plants such as ragweed, poke berries, dewberries, and blackberries will entice wildlife.

Innovative Farming Practices

After arriving home from visiting Jack Spigle's, I called Ned Jeter, conservation technician for MCSWCD, and a farmer from a family of rural landowners. I asked Jeter if the Commonwealth's farming community was aware of the many beneficial programs available.

"Some farmers are very skeptical of these programs," Jeter told me. "And I must admit that as a farmer myself, I too had doubts before I took this job. I just couldn't get over the fact that many of the programs took land out of use. How were my cattle going to get water if they were prevented from entering creeks? I was also skeptical of the benefits of riparian zones.

"But then I began to visit farms like Jack Spigle's and saw firsthand how these programs were working. A farmer who has developed projects like water fountains, riparian zones, and the paddock system of rotational grazing is able to put more cattle on less land and that translates into greater benefits and profits for the landowner. And the result is better for the environment and wildlife. What you have is truly a win-win situation."

"I also have found that all it takes is one or two farmers in an area to implement these practices, and then the whole farming community will look at the practices in a different light. I just need one or two movers and shakers to start things rolling," Jeter said.

Jeter detailed some of the additional innovative practices available. The 75 percent cost share and 25 percent tax credit program is available for a number of these projects while for others, landowners will receive incentive payments per acre.

Idle Land/Wildlife Option

Jeter described this as a very simple program to implement. If land has been row cropped, disked, or plowed or if small grains have been harvested, then the land can be left alone so that natural vegetation for wildlife can grow. This practice receives a one-time incentive payment.

Buffer Strip Cropping/Strip Cropping System

Instead of having one crop planted over an entire area, this program encourages farmers to sow two or three different plants that mature at different times in narrow rows. These strip crops are then harvested at different intervals so that soil erosion is reduced. That way, if the parcel is subject to erosion, the crops not harvested will serve as buffers for those which have just been removed. Jeter says, for example, that farmers could plant a parcel in strips of ladino clover, orchard grass, and kobe lespedeza and alternate those strips across the property instead of just having three large parcels of those plants.

Woodland Erosion Stabilization

When a landowner logs his property, this program enables him to stabilize the logging road and any steep slopes nearby. Switchgrass, clovers, and various warm and cool season grasses can be planted along the road or logging deck. Landowners who are hunters or allow hunting should especially look into this program as it is very beneficial for deer, turkey, and quail, as well as many songbirds and other nongame species.

Continuous No-till System

"Every time you turn soil, you can cause erosion," said Jeter. "And the ground can take several years to recover. With a no-till drill, which acts likes a serrated knife, the only soil that is disturbed is the exact spot where the seed enters the ground. After a small grain crop is harvested, a farmer can plant alfalfa or orchard grass as a cover crop. The plant residue from the small grain crop acts as ground cover for a second crop, thus reducing the amount of nonpoint source pollution."

For More Information

Reforestation of Erodible Crop and Pastureland

A very simple program that helps a landowner plant trees in, for example, riparian zones.

Farm Road/Heavy Traffic Animal Travel Lane Stabilization

"Let's say there's a creek on a farm, and, for whatever reason, the cattle have to go through it," said Jeter. "This program will help the landowner find a spot to create a lane that will only be about eight feet wide and has a gradual grade. Also, the lane will be created at a location without any shade so the animals won't linger in the stream. And to reduce erosion, we'll line the lane with different-sized stones."

Permanent Vegetative Cover on Critical Areas

This program is especially beneficial if a landowner has a barren hillside riddled with gullies. The hillside can be graded, limed, fertilized, and heavily seeded at twice the normal rate with plant species beneficial to wildlife.

Permanent Vegetative Cover on Cropland

This program enables the farmer to receive money not to plow/disk highly erodible land near streams. Jeter tries to encourage this program everywhere because taxpayers "get the best bang for their buck" when highly erodible land is removed from the planting schedule. To benefit from this program, farmers also have to plant a permanent crop such as orchard grass or a mixture of legumes. Jeter noted, "Fifty tons of soil per year can come off an acre of land near a stream. Water can move dirt like nothing else."

After the tour at Penn Farm, as we drove back to the barn, I remarked on how many projects Jack Spigle had going.

"Trying to make a farm better for wildlife is not just a one- or two-year deal," he replied. "It's a lifelong project."

Such is indeed the case, and hopefully many farmers will be able to implement many of the practices that Spigle and other creative, dedicated landowners have been able to do.

Part Two:

Enhancing the Experience

Chapter 7

Take a Child Fishing This Summer

One of the most enjoyable fishing trips I have ever experienced was the one my then eight-year-old son Mark and I took to land our family owns in Craig County, Virginia. We wade fished for smallmouth bass, rock bass, and redbreast sunfish along a tributary of the James River and afterward we gathered wood, built a fire, and roasted potatoes and skewered hot dogs.

I don't recall how many fish we caught that day, for the numbers do not really tell the story nor are they even important. What I remember most is how special it was to spend time with my son and share with him my passion for the outdoors.

But I also fondly remember how I instructed him to softly drag his feet across the bottom while wade fishing, how to lip a smallmouth bass and slide it back into the water, how to cook over a fire, and how it is important to clean up after oneself and thoroughly extinguish a fire before leaving a site. And I hope that when Mark, now in his twenties, has children of his own one day, he will instill in them some of the skills and values I have tried to pass on to him.

Like all states, Virginia boasts a number of lakes and rivers that make for fun family excursions. Here are some of the possible destinations.

Lakes

For lakes, Virginia's sporting families have many to choose from. The state's largemouth impoundment, 48,900-acre Buggs Island, is certainly a sound selection as it boasts one of the best populations of crappie in the entire United States. Buggs also harbors bluegills and channel catfish, two more species that often delight children. Buggs Island lies in south central Virginia and as such is within a three-hour drive of most of the state's population.

In north central Virginia, Lake Anna certainly deserves a look, and like Buggs Island, this Spotsylvania impoundment contains bluegills and crappie. Anna is also known for its largemouth bass and stripers.

Perhaps no section of the state offers as much family fishing potential as the Tidewater region does. Eastern Virginia does not have any large impoundments but what it does offer is plenty of small lakes from 50 to 2,000 acres. Many of these lakes contain members of the sunfish family, such as bluegills, redears, pumpkinseeds, and warmouths. Fetching destinations include lakes Prince, Western Branch, Cahoon, Kilby, Meade, and Speights Run.

Rivers

My favorite kind of angling involves floating one of Virginia's many quality upland or Piedmont rivers. These waterways feature smallmouths, rock bass, and redbreast sunfish. Smallmouths, of course, are the most difficult to catch of the trio, but, remember that many, if not most, kids would rather catch many fish than just a few large specimens. Redeyes and redbreasts are known for being accommodating in that area.

The James is a great choice for a destination as are such streams as the Rappahannock, Rapidan, Maury, Clinch, and North Fork of the Holston. The New is an outstanding waterway, but anglers should be aware that sections of the New, like every western waterway for that matter, contain some major rapids. However, the New hosts more whitewater than any other stream in the state.

Ponds

One of my early rites of passage as an angler was when I just earned my driver's license and was able to motor to farm ponds near my Salem home. My 1962 Ford Galaxy opened up a sporting world that I had only dreamed of, and big bucketmouths and bull bluegills became my quarry. Pond bluegills are among the most aggressive fish and even budding anglers typically have no problem catching as many as they want. More advanced youngsters can learn how to use minnow lures and soft plastic worms to fool the largemouths in these mini-impoundments.

Although ponds typically lie on private land, I have rarely experienced much difficulty gaining permission to fish them. Many landowners want the bluegills caught from their impoundments, as these

The author's son Mark with a smallmouth bass caught on a parent-child fishing excursion.

sunfish can quickly become overpopulated. And rare is the landowner who won't let an adult bring a child to fish, especially if that child is quite content to focus on bluegills by dangling a nightcrawler under a red-and-white bobber.

Tips for Fishing with Kids

When you take a kid fishing, you should have an entirely different set of priorities than when angling with a fellow adult. Here are some tips to keep in mind.

- Keep the outings short. My wife Elaine and I always let our children Mark and Sarah determine when it was time to quit fishing and head for home. Don't be surprised that your kids, especially if they are under six, will only want to fish for an hour or so before they want to engage in some other activity. Accommodate those desires; no kid should be forced to continue fishing.

- Bring along plenty of snacks. Our kids turned into eating machines when the family went on angling outings. Apples, bananas, peanut butter sandwiches, and granola bars should be available in abundance.

- Going fishing does not necessarily mean fishing the entire time. Every time Elaine and I went fishing with our son and daughter on the creek that lies on our Botetourt County land, the tikes would fish for a while then want to seine for crayfish, minnows, hellgrammites, and the other beasties that dwell in small streams. Our kids absolutely relished lifting up a seine with masses of squirming creatures within. Chances are that yours will, too.

- Don't forget to teach a few lessons about wildlife. Going fishing with your kids is a fun way to teach them about the great outdoors. It's not too soon to talk to your children about the importance of clean air and water and what stewardship is.

Chapter 8

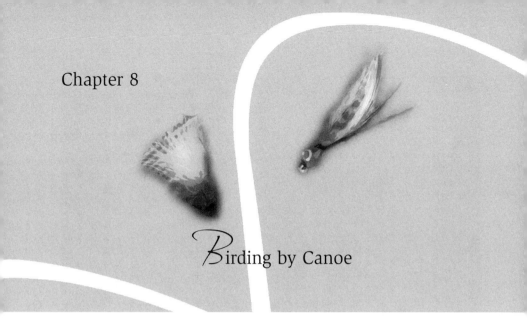

Birding by Canoe

As Kevin Hining, a fisheries biologist for the North Carolina Wildlife Resources Commission, and I launched our canoe on the South Fork of the New, the prognostications began.

"I predict 30, 35 tops," I said.

"That many? It's mid-July you know; how about 25?" replied Hining.

The final count was a heady 43, but that tally was not how many smallmouths we caught—although we did catch plenty of fish that day from this Tarheel State waterway. The figure refers to how many birds we either saw or heard as we paddled along.

Three of my most favorite outdoor pursuits are birding, canoeing, and fishing, so it's only natural that I came to combine them into exhilarating days afield—or perhaps *afloat* is a better word. Here are a few reasons why you may enjoy doing the same.

Spending Quality Time with Loved Ones

One of the best ways I know for couples to spend quality time together is to go on a canoe birding excursion down a nearby river. My wife Elaine and I are both school teachers and a marvelous way to reconnect with each other and decompress from a week in the classroom is to spend a Saturday floating the James River near our Virginia home.

For example, on one June junket down the James, we counted 33 species, and many avian males were still belting out their courtship serenades. We became so involved in trying to top 30 species that we forgot all about why Little Johnny at school refuses to do his

Birding by canoe is a great way for a family to enjoy time in the outdoors together.

homework. Comparable workaday cares, from whatever your vocation, will similarly disappear from your psyche as you and yours drift down a stream.

Another marvelous aspect of canoeing couples going bird watching is that this pastime gives them a chance to display their singular individual observation skills, yet at the same time work in tandem. For example, a recent behavioral study showed that men are better at seeing the big picture of an area whereas women perform better at spotting details. This translates into my probably being better able to recognize why a streamside habitat will likely produce, for instance, a yellow warbler. Meanwhile, Elaine is more likely to be the individual that first espies a yellow warbler.

I also seem better able than my spouse to pick out the individual song of a common yellowthroat from among the cacophony of bird music we hear as we drift along. Yet, conversely, I would wager that Elaine would be the first to spot the nest of the yellowthroat.

Canoe birding is a marvelous family activity, as well. When our son Mark was still in elementary school, we took him on birding float trips. Usually youngsters have a tendency to become quickly bored with any activity. But on a canoeing outing, a different vista awaits as you round every bend. And a whole different range of bird species awaits every time the canoe courses by a different kind of habitat.

Mark kept busy looking through a field guide for identification purposes, checking off species on a field card, gazing through binoculars, and helping paddle the canoe. The dreaded phrase "I'm bored" was never heard. I also believe that my son's passion for the outdoors and his concern for conservation issues stem from these early days afield.

Better Understanding Bird Habitats

Nothing will crystallize which habitats certain avian species prefer than to spend a day birding by boat. A stream flowing by any form of wildlife haunt creates the perfect edge-type habitat, and birds, as is true with many wildlife species, will often conduct much of their feeding, singing, and nesting activities streamside.

For instance, on one of my favorite James River float trips, an overgrown thicket exists on river left at the float's beginning. This is ideal white-eyed vireo surroundings, and from past experiences, I know to listen for this species' "chip-whee-oo-chick" every time I float by. I am also likely to hear the "drink your tea" tune from a towhee, the jumbled, disjointed whistles, squeaks, squawks, and scolds (and perhaps even a few mews and cackles) of a yellow-breasted chat, and the "tea-kettle-ettle-ettle" of a song sparrow.

Directly across the James from the thicket lies an overgrown field, and it too offers its own distinctive species. As I begin to paddle over to river right, I typically first detect the mellow, mellifluous "see-hear, see-year" of an Eastern meadowlark and then hear the clear trills— "twee-twee-twee"—of a field sparrow. If I can maneuver my canoe so that it hugs the shoreline, I have a real chance to hear the soft buzzy "tit-zeeeeeee" of a grasshopper sparrow deep in the field and perhaps even the distant sound of a bobwhite whistling its name over and over.

On this James getaway, the next habitat type is a mature forest that borders the James. Early and late in the day, I am likely to hear what I consider the most beautiful, enchanting sound in all of nature—the flutelike trills of a wood thrush. Gazing into the trees, I sometimes hear—and perhaps glimpse—a red-eyed vireo belting out his non-stop "now you see me, now you don't" phrases. In mature streamside stands, birders can also expect the "peter, peter, peter" of a tufted titmouse, the "su-dee-dee" of a Carolina chickadee, the nasal "yank, yank, yank" of a white-breasted nuthatch, and the "tuee, tuee, teeto" of a hooded warbler.

Many birdwatchers have a favorite bird that they relish seeing above all others, and for me, that species is a Carolina wren. I listen for the "wheedle, wheedle, wheedle" of the ever-inquisitive Carolina wren all along a river, as this reddish brown bundle of activity with its teetering body and jerking tail is likely to turn up just about everywhere. This aggressive bird is also likely to cast its buzzy alarm note as you drift by its territory.

Of course, some avian species tend to congregate in very specific habitats, even certain types of trees. A good example of this is the orchard oriole, which overwhelmingly seems to prefer mature streamside sycamores. Sometimes in mid- to late spring and well into summer, every third sycamore will seem to have an orchard oriole flitting about its treetop. Apparently, male orioles are able to fairly tolerate others of their sex in relatively close proximity. Listen for the oriole's robin-like "what cheer, what cheer" chorus.

In a very specific place on my float (although exceptions exist), I am also most likely to hear the three loud ringing notes of a Louisiana waterthrush, which it follows with a jumbled, descending warble. Especially look for waterthrushes where a briskly flowing tributary stream enters the main river.

Some species are more likely to be seen first, then heard, and not surprisingly these are the birds that feed and dwell along the water's edge or in water willow covered islets. Great blue and green herons are prime examples of the former, as they often can be observed wading along shallow stretches of a waterway. And if the wood thrush flaunts the best singing voice of any bird, there are few worse "singers" than the great blue and his loud guttural "honnk." When you pass islets, expect to see red-winged blackbirds and spotted sandpipers.

Choosing Binoculars for Canoe Birding

Bill Hunley, a member of the Roanoke Valley (Virginia) Bird Club, is one of the best canoe birders I know. He emphasizes that boat-bound birders should demand binoculars with two traits.

"Waterproofed and low power are what you should look for," said Hunley. "Sooner or later, a canoe birder is going to either drop his binoculars into the water or get them wet when a wave splashes into the boat. I also recommend that binoculars have a flotation strap

Keeping Things Afloat

About 1990, I made the most prudent purchase I have ever made concerning any of my many outdoor pursuits. For about $35, I bought a Pelican Mini S Case, which is about the size of a lunchbox. Over the years, I have obtained a number of other Pelican cases and have found them ideal for storing canoe birding essentials such as binoculars, cameras, field guides, and snacks. These cases have also saved me money.

For example, once on an April float down the James, a friend and I overturned a canoe, and in the cold water we were barely able to swim to shore. My friend desperately wanted to retrieve his boat while I was just as frantic to recover my $1,100 camera, which was inside the Pelican Mini S Case. For about 300 yards, we ran down the shoreline, following the bobbing, upside-down canoe.

At last, the craft eddied out and we waded into shallow water to rescue our possessions. When we flipped the canoe over, underneath it was my Pelican case with my camera inside—dry and undamaged. I always keep my camera inside the case, except, obviously, when I am taking pictures. And I always store binoculars in a case when my canoe approaches a rapid of any level of intensity.

Finally, I recommend that canoe birders always wear a lifejacket—even during the heat of summer and even in calm water. My wife and I once overturned in (of all places) a backwater pool when I stood up to stretch and she happened simultaneously to lean over the side. Water-related accidents can happen at any time. For more information on Pelican Products, contact the company at www.pelican.com, (800) 473-5422, or (310) 326-4700.

attached, which, in the long run, can save you a lot of money should you drop your binoculars overboard in deep water.

"Waterproofed binoculars have usually been tested to withstand water seepage to a certain depth, often two meters. They also have their entire interior filled with nitrogen, which keeps them from fogging inside, as well. The addition of nitrogen also makes them dust-proof."

The Virginian defines low power binoculars as those that have a maximum power of 7x or 8x. It's just so hard, he said, to hold 9x and 10x models and glass a bird high in the treetops when a canoe is rocking back and forth. And the extra weight inherent in more powerful optics can be very tiring for a birder's neck, especially a person who enjoys venturing forth on day-long excursions.

Over the past few years, the price of waterproof binoculars has actually decreased, continued Hunley. He said that many outdoor catalogs carry quality models that sell for between $200 and $300. In the past, birders have had to spend as much as $500. One of the reasons for this price decrease has been the birding community's demand for well-made waterproof optics. Finally, concluded Hunley, although water-resistant binoculars do offer some protection and are cheaper, strongly consider paying a few dollars more and purchasing waterproof versions.

Maneuvering Your Canoe

In order to maximize the birding-by-boat experience, you will need to implement a few canoe positioning strategies. For example, if you want to enjoy good looks at such waterfowl as mallards and wood ducks, be sure to maneuver your craft tight to an outside bend. These species tend to forage close to the shoreline, especially outside bends, and will likely flush when you are far away unless you cautiously approach their positions. The shyness of mallards and woodies is in marked contrast to the studied indifference of Canada geese, which will often permit canoe birders to come quite close to them.

Rapids are another important consideration when planning a birding by boat getaway. I strongly advise birders to avoid sections with Class III rapids, often defined as being difficult, intense rapids, possibly with standing waves and boulders that demand quick maneuvering. Class II rapids are less dangerous, but these often feature pronounced drops in the stream bottom and scattered boulders. Beginning paddlers should not undertake excursions that contain Class IIs and above.

A Class I rapid typically presents little danger, but I must confess that Mark and I once overturned our Dagger Legend in a Class I because we were paying more attention to fishing and birding than a mid-river rock that lay ahead. Caution and vigilance are advised at all times.

Birding by canoe is a superlative way to pursue our passion for birds and the outdoors. And that time afloat is even more enjoyable if we are able to spend it with loved ones.

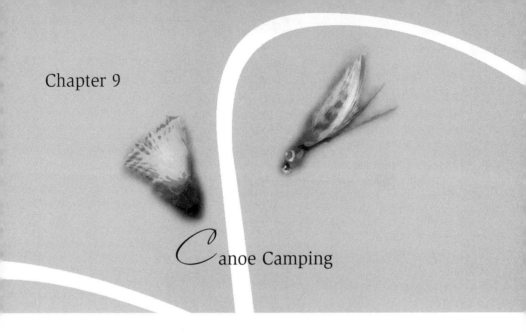

Chapter 9

Canoe Camping

The canoe camping excursion that my wife Elaine and I took down the Rapidan River on June 24 and 25 in 1989 is one that will long live in infamy in our family outdoor chronicles. Late in the afternoon of our initial day, we paddled up to a point where the beach was sandy and lay convenient to the river's edge. Elaine and I deemed the sand a perfect place to spend the night, as the sand would be a soft place to pitch our tent, and we could hear the water gently lapping at the shoreline all night.

After we built the traditional campfire on the beach, my wife and I shared a relaxing few hours before turning in. But upon entering our tent, we found that water had already seeped through the cheap floor fabric and that our sleeping bags were damp. Around midnight, a thunderstorm hit, and the roof of our tent began leaking unmercifully. Two hours later, as the storm continued unabated, the water that had been gently lapping against the beach now came rudely slapping against our tent.

Elaine and I were too scared to go back to sleep, and we spent the rest of the night anxiously eyeing the rising Rapidan. By dawn the river was muddy and still rising, so we decided to paddle quickly to the confluence of the Rapidan and Rappahannock and then the eight miles to the take-out at Motts Landing. At the confluence's rock garden, our canoe hit a rock, overturning us and sending much of our gear to the bottom of the river—we had neglected to tie down some of our possessions and hadn't bothered to bring along a dry bag.

Midmorning, we reached Motts, but not before being further terrified by more thunderstorms and the continually rising water. Safely home the next day, Elaine and I watched the news where a broadcaster proclaimed that the Rappahannock and Rapidan had both reached flood stage.

The preceding was a textbook example of how not to go canoe camping on any waterway. Craig Fields, who lives in Montross, Virginia, and works for the Gun Owners of America, has canoe camped across the Commonwealth as well as on a number of other rivers in other states and on the Boundary Waters. In short, Craig pointed out that Elaine and I made a litany of poor decisions on our Rapidan junket.

First, sandy beaches are terrible places to pitch a tent. Sand seems to seek out all kinds of gear from fishing reels to the night's dinner. Sand also holds water extremely well, as the bottom of our tent proved that misbegotten night on the Rapidan. And finally, Craig noted that sandy beaches are usually very close to water.

On a summertime float down the Maury several summers ago, Craig showed me how to select an overnight spot. We pulled up to a mid-river island that consisted of pebble-sized rocks and that featured a point that rose some 15 yards above the water line. At the top of the point, we found a level campsite that also provided good cross ventilation—necessary to disperse our scent so that a host of winged beasties could not as easily track us down. A pebble/gravel beach doesn't hold water or abrade gear and its level status makes for good sleeping. And choosing a site well above the water line like Craig did just makes common sense.

Sleeping Well

I have spent too many semi-sleepless nights on the Old Dominion's rivers, but after a sound repose in Craig's tent that night on the Maury, I am sure I won't anymore. His basic floor plan is to first place a tarp, which is larger than the floor, inside the tent. That way should any water find its way in through the floor bottom, all gear and human occupants will be above the liquid. Decisions concerning sleeping pads and bags come next.

"Way more than one-half of your sleeping comfort comes from whether or not you purchase the right kind of sleeping pad," said Craig. "It is folly to buy less than a full-length, self-inflating pad. Even mine (and I'm only five feet, six inches) is six feet long. The thicker the pad is, the more comfortable it will be. But the more it will weigh, and the bulkier it will be, as well. One inch or one and a half inches is about right for canoe camping. Backpackers should purchase something less thick, but never less than half an inch. My recommendation: one and a half inches."

"If the cover has a slick feel to it, and you are a restless sleeper, you and your sleeping bag can slide off the pad like eggs coming off a Teflon pan," he continued. "Most [of the] better brands nowadays feature a low-slip shell."

Craig Fields, shown here enjoying a riverside meal that he cooked, is an expert on canoe camping.

He believes that many people obtain sleeping bags that are far too warm for river camping, especially in Southern states. A good three-season bag is rated at +25 degrees Fahrenheit. Lining is another important consideration. Nylon lining can be quite sweaty while soft flannel lining is heavy and bulky. A way around this problem is to purchase a bag with a nylon lining and then bring along a cotton sheet or sleeping bag liner "to ward off the stickiness."

Of course, the purchase of a tent is a major consideration. Craig believes that the tent manufacturers wildly overestimate the number of people that can sleep comfortably within their products. A good rule of thumb is that if, for example, two people are on an expedition, they should bring a tent described as "four-person" (which typically has a floor size of 7'6" by 7'6" and a weight of 7 ½ pounds or so). If an individual plans to sleep by himself, a two-person tent (which typically has a floor size of 5' by 7'6" and a weight of 5 pounds or so) will have acceptable space.

Craig strongly emphasizes that the foremost qualification of a tent is that its seams are factory taped. This action ensures more than any other that the tent will not leak. Next, select one that is free-standing, such as a dome or modified A-frame. Given the vagaries of an island's composition, canoe campers might not be able to stake a tent completely down.

Aluminum tent poles are yet another important consideration; Craig relates that fiberglass models too easily break. Finally, consider buying tents that are flame retardant and feature multicoated, waterproof nylon. Tents, sleeping bags, and pads all need to be transported in quality dry bags. Stuff sacks alone, even high-dollar compression sacks, do not offer sufficient protection from the elements. Dry bags are a must, but do note, explains Craig, that sleeping bags should be stuffed, not rolled, as doing so lessens bulk immediately. All loose gear, like things not needed for activities such as birding or fishing, should be tied into the canoe. This is something else that Elaine and I learned on our ill-fated Rapidan ramble as we watched gear either sink to the bottom or float away.

Dining Out

Remember that campfire that Elaine and I made on the sandy point? As we scooted away from the island, I noted how unsightly the ring was, as were the other ones that previous voyagers had made. Once again, Craig Fields offers a better way. After we set up the tent during our Maury getaway, Craig had me dig a rectangular trench (large enough for a cooking grate (with diamond shaped holes to keep food from slipping through). I poured charcoal into the trench and positioned the grate so that it overlapped. After the coals had been burning for awhile, Craig cut up some potatoes into fairly small pieces, added some butter, and double wrapped the "tater bombs" in heavy-duty foil. While they were cooking, he placed venison tenderloin and a variety of fresh vegetables on skewers.

I rarely have experienced a dinner so scrumptious anywhere—and never on a canoe camping trek have I supped so well. The next morning, Craig had me fill in the trench, leaving the clean white ashes underneath to recycle into the substrate. Except for a matted space where the tent had been, no one could tell that humans had spent the night. And the skewers cleaned up much easier and faster than any frying pan and were much lighter, as well.

Craig advises that evening dinners should be the major meal for the day—and a social function as well—especially if multiple paddlers undertake a trip. He and I strongly agree that breakfast and lunch should be brief, do-it-yourself affairs, so as not to cut into fishing, bird watching, nature photography, or whatever activity an individual enjoys while on a river.

Gear List for Canoe Camping

1. One mess kit (each component with copper bottoms, for longevity) per person.

2. Life jackets. I wear one at all times, no matter how warm the temperature is or how mildly a river flows.

3. Water purifier.

4. Headlamps and flashlights.

5. Spare batteries.

6. First aid kit.

7. Eating utensils and short-handled metal tongs for cooking.

8. Cell phone (if an emergency should arise).

9. Spare clothing. Craig strongly recommends that no cotton clothing be brought, with the possible exception of an old T-shirt or two. Mesh-lined nylon shorts are fast drying, cotton garb is not. I always wear pants, long sleeved shirts, and a baseball style hat to protect me against the sun and insects. Sunglasses are a must.

10. Bailing sponge.

11. Bungee cords.

12. Toiletry kit (including biodegradable soap).

13. Lockback knife.

14. Lighters and matches.

15. Duct tape.

16. Food (personal choice). For breakfasts and lunches, my favorite canoe camping foods are apples, bagels, energy bars, and tuna in a pouch. Craig relishes hot chocolate and peanut butter and jelly sandwiches.

Fishing Gear

Craig emphasizes that fishing gear is another personal choice situation, but he and I also agree that light-weight pack rods or fly rods are of little practicality for the serious angler. While canoe campers may want to be conservative concerning space and weight of camping and cooking gear, both Craig and I advocate bringing along our full complement of fishing gear.

For me, that can mean a medium heavy baitcaster, two medium heavy spinning rods, a medium action spinning rod, and an 8 ½-foot bass bug taper long rod. In front of me in a canoe, I position four hard plastic mini-tackle boxes, each containing a different category of baits. One box contains soft plastics; another, topwaters; a third, crankbaits and spinnerbaits; and the last, fly patterns. I pair the soft plastic baits with the baitcaster and one of the medium heavy spinning rods, the topwaters are matched with the medium action spinning outfit, and the other lures generally go with the other medium heavy spinning rod. I see no use in bringing full-sized tackle boxes on treks down our rivers, regardless of whether I am canoe camping or not.

Possible Trips

Public camping areas or campgrounds occur infrequently along many rivers. In North Carolina along the New River, for example, exists the New River State Park where canoe campers have designated areas where they can spend the night and enjoy facilities. Individuals can paddle to these waysides and spend the night there. Perhaps such places and services will one day exist along some of Virginia's waterways, but none do now so far as I know.

Thus, a canoe camper basically has four options. He can attempt to contact a land owner along a river before or during a trip and ask for permission to spend the night on that individual's property. Second, the overnight voyager can select trips on rivers that have public land along one or both banks. For instance, I have camped out in the George Washington National Forest while on trips down the South Fork of the Shenandoah. Third, canoe campers can contact canoe liveries, which often own or rent land along rivers, and, for a fee, arrange to spend the night on the property of such a business. Lastly, paddlers can spend the night at mid-river islands that are not privately owned. Campers can locate these islands by studying maps of our rivers.

Elaine's and my Rapidan River excursion in June 1989 was so disastrous that my spouse would not go canoe camping with me for several years—and who could blame her? Use the tips offered by veteran canoe camper Craig Fields so that you and yours can have a safe, enjoyable journey down the wonderful rivers in our state.

Chapter 10

*E*leven Must-Have Items for the Canoe Camper ...
For No More than $200

The inspiration for a canoe camping gear story came when I received a gift certificate for $100 from a sporting goods store. Prowling the aisles of the establishment made me ponder just how much paraphernalia I could possibly purchase.

The point is that by spending relatively little (no more than $100 to $200), canoeists who enjoy fishing, birding, exploring, or outdoor photography (or all four as I do) can turn their day trips into overnight adventures. That is, of course, if these individuals already own the bare minimum for their pursuits, such as a tent, sleeping bag and pad, and fishing gear (for an angler) or binoculars and field guides (for a birder).

My good friend Craig Fields of Montross, Virginia, is a hardcore canoe camper that regularly undertakes week-long treks. He offers the following tidbits of gear advice; note that most of these items could also prove useful for land lubbers who prefer to do their camping far from waterways.

1: Dry Bag

"You can never have too many dry bags, and if any of your river tripping gear isn't already assigned to a dry bag, get that done first," said Craig. "The only things of mine that I don't put into a dry bag are a cooking grate and fishing gear."

Dry bags are essential for a canoe camper but handy for the general camper as well; they make excellent places to store food, clothes, and toiletries in both situations. I also employ dry bags as scent-free storage compartments for my deer hunting camouflage.

2: Primary Light Source

A Craig Fields favorite is his Coleman double mantle propane unit with case. For years I was too tight to spend even a few dollars for any kind of artificial light. But that night my wife and I spent on a rapidly rising river where we had to head for higher ground freed me from my excessive thriftiness. A Coleman propane unit can easily send forth luminosity across a camping area and cheer the disposition of everyone.

3: A D-cell Tent Lantern

If canoe campers desire more light, they can add a D-cell tent lantern. For a tent light, I bought a Coleman Floating Krypton Lantern; the buoyancy of this item is an added benefit.

One of the great joys of canoe or regular camping is reclining inside a tent and replaying the events of the day with good friend or a loved one. Another sublime camping pleasure is our having the time to read a good book or some other form of literature. For both situations, a tent lantern adds to the ambience.

4: Headlamp

A headlamp is another gear piece that I refused to purchase for years. But headlamps are marvelous things to have when one needs to walk, for example, down to the river to fish or search for more firewood. In fact, Craig recommends purchasing two so one can be loaned out or used as a backup.

The Little Things

Craig suggests that campers stock up or have replacements for what he calls the "little things." These include items such as: first aid kit supplies, batteries, bug dope, hand sanitizers, bandanas, quick-dry camp towels, mess kit components, propane cylinders, and lantern mantles.

Craig Fields setting up a riverside camp. Fields believes that a number of inexpensive items that exist can add to the camping experience.

Craig also clued me in on another attribute of these light suppliers. When bow hunters climb tree stands in the dark, they will find that a headlamp enables them to have both hands free as they ascend—an important safety consideration.

5: Mini Shovel

More and more campers of all persuasions are practicing the "leave no trace" ethic. An important tool in accomplishing this goal is a tri-fold entrenching tool for fire pits and the burial of human waste. For example, on an outing with Craig several years ago, while he was setting up the tent, he instructed me to use a mini shovel to build a fire pit.

I then placed coals inside the depression, and it was there that we cooked our dinner. Afterward, I doused the fire with water, and the next morning (after determining that the fire was completely out) we covered the pit with soil. As we paddled away from the campsite, no one could have ascertained that we had spent the night there.

6: Cooking Grate

One could, I suppose, make do with two rocks and a frying pan strategically placed over a fire pit, but for higher class outdoor cooking, a heavy duty grate receives the nod.

"A camp grate must have legs reinforced with rails at the bottom, not four spikes," insisted Craig. "And it should be large enough to hold lots of skewers and have no openings greater than, say, half an inch. A diamond pattern or circular hole pattern are about the only worthwhile choices. Standard parallel grills are too chancy, often allowing food to fall through their openings."

7: Cooler

Craig Fields suggests one of the newer "max" coolers that holds ice for five days. He prefers the 54 quart size for canoe camping. Of course, Craig often goes on week-long excursions with his coolers. Readers who intend to go on paddling treks of shorter durations can downsize accordingly.

8: Rain Gear

Concerning this category, Craig is quite blunt.

"New rain gear is never out of order," he asserted. "Waterproof/breathable is a must—no coated nylon."

Coated nylon is a cheap option; however, this fabric offers extremely poor protection from precipitation. Campers of all kinds can become hypothermic at any time of the year, not just during the winter. Why risk this painful and dangerous condition? I once experienced a mild case of hypothermia during a July day trip on the New River. A heavy downpour coupled with a friend's and my canoe, overturning in a rapid.

The Magical Multi-Tool Knife

For a multi-tool knife, Craig Fields favors the traditional and famous Swiss Army Knife, specifically the Swiss Champ. He also speaks highly of tool knives made by Leatherman, while I wouldn't trade my Buck tool knife.

"If your tool knife doesn't at least have both scissors and pliers, you need a more expensive and/or larger one," emphasized Craig.

Campers should realize that tool knives are not cheap; a quality one can cost $75 or more.

After struggling to paddle to the take-out while enduring intense bouts of shivering, I finally arrived at the vehicle and turned the heater on high and, shivering, drove all the way home with the heat on full blast. The air temperature outside: 82 degrees. Imagine what could happen to a human body during, for example, a spring rainstorm if the canoeists are dressed in light cotton clothing (which retains moisture) and are wearing nylon rain jackets.

9: Camp Stove

I have relished consuming Craig's skewered veggie and venison shish kabob creations for dinner and consider them the ideal food to cook over a grate. But canoe campers and others may also find a single or double burner propane camp stove useful. Craig relates that overnight adventurers can add considerable variety to their menus by bringing along a stove.

For example, on one trip I used a single burner to cook a hearty breakfast of organic oatmeal laced with bananas, dried blueberries, and cranberries. Add in some cinnamon and vanilla flavoring and you have a breakfast that is guaranteed to give you the energy to accomplish some serious paddling. Rice, soups, and even pudding can come from a propane burner, as can a host of other dishes.

Note: this item will likely be the priciest one on our gear list. Coleman, for instance, offers a dazzling variety of single and double propane camp stoves with the most inexpensive ones beginning around $25.

10: Dining Fly

A dining fly may or may not be considered essential, but Craig believes this item adds a nice touch to an outing. He likes to extend a fly from the tent entrance out over the cooking and dining area, a particularly good thing to have done if rain starts to fall. On one such outing of ours, heavy precipitation did fall, and we would have been miserable scooting back and forth between the tent and fire—if there had not been a fly protecting the area.

Craig recommends high quality nylon, saying it is better than polyethylene (the ubiquitous blue tarp) but notes that nylon is much more expensive.

11: River Sandals

Tennis shoes might be a popular choice, but Craig emphasizes that they are not a wise one. Rubber-based shoes have a tendency to smell, harbor germs, and take a long time to dry and can lead to a variety of ailments such as athlete's foot. His suggestion: river sandals or at least mesh-topped water shoes.

Also worthy of consideration are mesh-lined river shorts or pants. The veteran camper urges folks to consider doing away with cotton underwear and socks as well, as cotton adsorbs moisture and dries extremely slowly, "not to mention just being plain uncomfortable."

Upon Craig's suggestion, I bought a pair of nylon pants and was very pleased with my purchase. Periodically, I like to beach a canoe and wade fish and/or utilize binoculars to search for riparian zone dwelling birds like orchard orioles and Louisiana waterthrush. In the past a quick wading detour would have left my cotton pants wet for the rest of the day and even through the next morning. In contrast, the sun will dry my nylon pants in about 30 minutes.

For More Information

- Bob's Red Mill:
  www.bobsredmill.com
  I order all my organic oatmeal from this company, which also has a variety of other "good to take camping" products such as hot and cold cereals, soups, nuts, and dried fruits.
- Buck Knives:
  www.buckknives.com
- Canoe Camping USA:
  www.canoe-camping.org
  This site offers a variety of tips for planning a trip.
- Coleman Company:
  www.coleman.com
  Coleman offers a complete line of camping gear, as well as gear checklists.
- Leatherman:
  www.leatherman.com
- Swiss Army Knife:
  www.swissarmy.com

Craig Fields' Shish Kabob Shore Supper Recipe

○ Marinate venison tenderloin for several hours in Italian dressing.

○ Wait until charcoal or wood has turned gray, then skewer slices of tenderloin.

○ When meat has slightly browned, add vegetables to skewers. (Possibilities include tomatoes, peppers, onions, leaks, potatoes, squash, and zucchini.)

○ Cook to desired doneness.

○ For an even heartier meal, at least 40 minutes before beginning tenderloin, place potatoes wrapped in double foil in coals. Craig likes to place slabs of real butter inside foil. Cooking time depends on size of potato.

Chapter 11

The Worst Guides I've Ever Met

Ah, the glamorous life of an outdoor writer, gadding about the countryside, going fishing and hunting with professional guides. Actually, that common perception is not quite accurate. Yes, we do venture afield quite a bit, and many of our excursions are memorable. However, some of the guides and the junkets they took me on were straight out of the twilight zone. Here are my most nightmarish trips.

The Turkey Guide Who Did Not Permit Calling

On opening day of spring gobbler season one year, I went with a guide who had been recommended by a nationally known hunting celebrity. The guide and I arose early and journeyed to a farm.

Just before sunrise, I took out a slate caller and began to run sandpaper across it.

"Put that away," he said sharply.

"Why?" was my surprised reply.

"I don't want to attract other hunters," he snapped.

"How are we going to attract turkeys then?" I asked politely.

No answer was forthcoming, but I can tell you that we sat in the woods for the next two hours like proverbial knots on a log. After that time elapsed, the guide told me that it was time to quit because the "birds weren't cooperating." I later learned that the nationally known celebrity who had recommended this individual had never met him, let alone gone hunting with him. This affair led me to develop a policy to never mention a guide's name in print unless I had gone afield with him. In fact, it is a good policy for all of us to check out a guide (ask plenty of questions and request recommendations) before agreeing to a trip.

The Turkey Guide Who Tried to Call in a Mowing Machine

At least one turkey guide I went with would have been better off if he hadn't tried to call. The two of us had been hunting for several hours without any luck and were on our way back to the car. Suddenly the guide uttered a terse command.

"Sit down, I hear a hen and I bet she's got a gobbler with her," he whispered.

I strained my ears in the direction he pointed, but all I could hear was a soft, rhythmic, and mechanical "click, click, click" about a hundred yards away. While hunched against a tree, I could detect that every minute or so, the sound would appear to come closer, but then it would progressively become less audible for the next minute.

Meanwhile, my guide was beside himself with excitement and engaged in a rapturous outpouring of yelps, clucks, and purrs. After about 15 minutes, I could endure matters no longer, so sure I was that a turkey was not uttering those clicks. I arose and began walking toward the nearby field.

"Sit down," the guide croaked in a harsh whisper. "You're going to spook a big gobbler."

I ignored his instructions and, arriving at the field edge, I saw a mowing machine cutting hay up and down a field - the machine was the obvious source of the noise and the back-and-forth circuit was the reason why the sounds appeared louder and softer from time to time. I questioned him on why he would try to call in a mowing machine. His response?

"A gobbler had been on its way until the mower scared it off," he said.

The Guide Who Touted His Gourmet Food

I once visited a hunting lodge, in large part because a brochure had touted the establishment's gourmet food. Unfortunately, the dinner menu was as follows: one hot dog per person (the frank was deep-fried in some very dark and loathsome looking grease), macaroni and cheese (one serving), rolls (a limit of two), and orange juice (the juice was very watery and clear and obviously had been watered down).

I did not have the courage to sample the frankfurter, I can't stand macaroni, and I asked for water instead of juice. The next morning I was ravenous with hunger, but all that was offered were the leftover dinner

Don't get stuck with an inadequate guide. Make sure to research your guide ahead of time. Ask plenty of questions and request recommendations before agreeing to a trip, or you may regret your choice.

rolls and watery orange juice. This time, I couldn't keep my mouth shut and sweetly inquired about his clients' usual responses to the menu.

"You know, I get a lot of complaints about my food," said the outfitter. "I can't imagine why."

I can.

The Guide Who Advertised Deluxe Accommodations

I was once convinced to visit an outfitter who, over the phone, raved about his spacious lodge and its deluxe accommodations. Upon my arrival, the fellow took me to what looked on the outside to be a smallish chicken coop.

After entering the structure, I immediately saw the nesting boxes, which to the outfitter's credit, had been freshly painted. I was more than a little surprised when he told me that this was his "spacious" lodge, considering that the chicken boxes outnumbered the cots twelve to four. The "deluxe" accommodations consisted of two chairs and a bathroom.

That night, the temperature was expected to dip quite low. When I asked for a blanket, I was given only one. I wrapped myself in that blanket, because, as deluxe as the accommodations were, they did not include a heating unit. I shivered all night long.

To make matters worse, the guide awoke me extremely early the next morning, at least an hour earlier than I felt was necessary. I soon found out why. After breakfast, we piled into his car and, incredibly, began driving around in circles. The third time we passed a stop sign near his house, I asked the gent what in the world he was doing.

"I'm trying to get you confused so you won't know where we are going," he said. "I don't want you moving in on my hunting spots."

I tried to explain that I lived many miles away and that it would be ridiculous for me to return and trespass on his properties. He was not convinced, however, and every few minutes we would once again pass the stop sign.

Finally, we arrived at our destination.

"Does this place have many turkeys?" I asked.

"Don't know," he mumbled. "I've never hunted it before."

Recovering from my amazement at that statement, I asked him if he had any gobblers located anywhere.

"Yep," he replied.

"Can we go there?" I inquired.

"Nope, got to save those gobblers for some clients coming in next week," he said.

Not surprisingly, we didn't hear any turkeys. I also declined the invitation to spend another night in the spacious lodge.

The Guide Who Housed His Clients in an Abandoned School Bus

As bad as the sleeping conditions in the chicken coop were, in all fairness I would have to say they were superior to those I endured on another trip. After a guide's glowing report about his accommodations, I booked a trip.

Upon arrival at his establishment, I was astonished to learn that his "lodge" was an abandoned school bus that he had "fixed up." I spent the night sprawled across row 10, an experience I would not wish upon my worst enemy. The guide awoke me at 3 a.m. and for the next hour, I watched him drink coffee.

Finally, we left the bus and drove 90 minutes to our destination. We pulled up to the "farm" at daylight, and I asked him how many acres we would be hunting on.

"Five," he replied.

We walked down to the end of a gravel road and back, and the hunt was over- taking all of ten minutes.

The Trout Guide Who Raved about the Weather and Fishing

One April, I decided to enjoy some trout fishing and called a guide whose service I had seen listed. He enthusiastically told me that the weather was great, water levels were perfect, and the trout were biting.

Arriving the next day, I found that the river was flooding, the meteorologist was calling for more rain, and that the fisheries department had no plans to stock the stream because a logging company had clear-cut the watershed. I angrily asked the outfitter why he had not been forthright about matters.

"If I had told you the truth, you wouldn't have come," he said.

The Fishing Guide Who Boasted about his Boating Expertise

I once went fishing with a guide who, over the phone, bragged about his boat-handling skills. Upon launching his craft, I spotted two boulders, two feet apart, just 50 yards downstream.

I warned the guide about the boulders, but he told me that we would run between them. I didn't do well in arithmetic in school, but I know that a basic law of math is that three-foot-wide johnboats shall not pass between boulders two feet apart. Realizing that a crash was imminent, I gathered up my fishing rods and tackle and prepared for impact.

We struck the rocks, the boat began to sink, and I watched the guide's fishing rods slide beneath my feet and over the bow. I could have saved his gear but was not inclined to do so. Being dumped into 50-degree water seems to bring out the worst in me.

The Guide Who Refused to Quit Fishing

My wife Elaine and I once fished with a guide who throughout the morning actually did a fairly competent job. Elaine and I both caught fish, and by noon requested to be taken in, especially since storm clouds had appeared.

We both put away our fishing gear, but then the guide took his out, saying that he wanted to "take advantage of the front." The sky continued to darken, and then lightening started to strike around us. And our guide kept fishing.

By the time we arrived at the guide's van, we were all soaked, Elaine and I were scared from the lightening and thunder, and the guide had not caught a single fish during "the front." For Elaine, the day was made perfect when the outfitter told her to sit on the floor of his filthy van.

"But first, you gotta move some oil rags out of the way," he said.

The best news for readers is that all of the guides mentioned in this story went out of business. Can't imagine why, can you?

Part Three:
Summertime Smallmouth Fishing

Chapter 12

Five Can't-Miss Patterns
for Summertime Smallmouths

Dedicated lake largemouth anglers often speak about developing patterns on their favorite body of water, and the truth is that much of the time on impoundments, pattern fishing is the most logical plan of attack. Hardcore river smallmouth anglers also recognize the benefit of pattern fishing, for stream smallies likewise hold in certain defined areas where fishermen can entice them with certain lures and flies, especially from mid-spring through mid-fall. Here, then, are five can't-miss warm weather patterns for flowing water bronzebacks.

Deep Water Ledges, Soft Plastic Baits, and Subsurface Selections

In my opinion, the most consistent pattern throughout the warm weather period is the deep water ledge and soft plastic one. Several years ago a friend and I went on an all day excursion on Virginia's James River, covering almost 18 miles. At daybreak just after launching, we came to our first structure situation—a spot where two limestone ledges barely dimpled the surface of the water, but the drop-off between them extended into at least six feet of water.

My friend dropped a plastic crayfish into the recesses and soon afterward derricked out a three-pounder. Over the course of the next ten hours, we caught and released about 30 smallies between 12 and 21 inches, the vast majority of them coming from ledges and falling for soft plastic baits.

Soft Plastic Selections
- Worms: 6-inch Mister Twister Phenom and Zoom U-Tail.
- Crayfish: 4-inch Mister Twister Poc-it Dad and Venom Clickin' Craw.
- Tubes: 3-inch Venom Finesse Salt Tube and 4-inch Super Do, Case Tube, Yamamoto Tube.

- Salamanders: 6-inch Zoom Super Salty Lizard and Berkley Gulp Lizard.
- Mad Toms/Creature Baits: Venom 3-inch Mad Tom, Case Mad Tom and Hellgrammite, Yamamoto Hula Grub.

Subsurface Selections (sizes 2 to 8)
- Woolly Buggers
- Marabou Leeches
- Clouser Minnows
- Clouser Golden Shiners
- Whitlock's Softshell Crayfish
- Muddler Minnows

Insider Tips

Use ¼-ounce bullet sinkers to help baits sink into the inner sanctums of ledges. Pair weights with Fat Gap 2/0 or 3/0 Daiichi Bleeding Bait Hooks. Long rodders should use sink tip line and split shot.

Regarding line, Duane Richards, who operates the fishing site www.duanerichards.proboards23.com, has strong opinions. "There are more good choices than ever before," he says. "But mono is not the best choice anymore for soft plastic fishing. My favorite is Hi-Vis Power Pro 6/20 because it has no line twist ever and the strong hook sets are phenomenal. It has such sensitivity that it can make a $5 rod feel like a $70 one."

Conversely, Dave Maurice prefers Yo-Zuri Hybrid, a nylon and fluorocarbon blend, in 8-pound test. The noted Ohio River angler likes Yo-Zuri for the same reasons that Richards prefers Power Pro.

Shoreline Laydowns, Topwater Lures, and Fly Poppers

One of the best and most exciting aspects of river smallmouth angling is that a topwater bite not only lasts throughout most of the warm water season but also throughout the day almost every day. The most consistent place to experience this action is the shoreline.

For example, several years ago while on the New River, which flows through North Carolina and both Virginias, I began the day by tossing a Rapala Skitter Prop to partially submerged trees extending out from the shoreline. Several times I could see the smallmouths "waking" behind the

The author's wife Elaine displaying a smallmouth caught on the James River. There are at least five can't-miss patterns for summertime smallmouths.

bait, crushing it before the prop bait either left the confines of the tree or before where the shade gave way to sunlight.

As the day progressed and the shade enveloping the shoreline shrank, the smallmouths became more concentrated along shoreline wood, but the bass remained aggressive. Downed trees lying perpendicular to the shoreline became more productive than the ones at a right angle to the bank. Indeed, some of the most explosive surface smashes came at high noon when the shaded area along the bank extended outward only a foot or so.

And on a trip one summer to a Virginia creek, I caught nearly 20 fish in less than three hours on just one topwater pattern: the Tim Holschlag Big Blockhead. Indeed, the fly was so successful at drawing strikes from smallies that I never considered employing a different pattern.

Interestingly, Holschlag, who was with me that day, affixed his creation to my line by means of a loop knot. He believes that this knot allows the fly much greater freedom of movement as the angler pops it along.

Topwater Choices
- Prop baits: Heddon Tiny Torpedo, Bill Lewis Rat-L-Top, Phillips Crippled Killer, Rapala Skitter Prop.
- Chuggers: Rebel Pop-R, Berkley Frenzy Popper, Cabela's Fisherman Series Top Popper, Rapala Skitter Pop.
- Stick Baits: Heddon Zara Spook, Storm Chug Bug, Lucky Craft Sammy, Berkley Frenzy Walker.
- Poppers: Sneaky Pete Popper, Tim Holschlag Big Blockhead, Pencil Popper, and Walt's Poppers.

Insider Tips

When the shoreline laydown/shadow/topwater bite is ongoing, consider keeping at least four rods rigged with topwaters. For example, I will tie on a prop bait on one rod, a chugger on another, either a hard or soft plastic jerkbait on the third, and a Sneaky Pete Popper or Big Blockhead on another. Don't leave a bank until you have worked all lures /flies in and around the shade. Sometimes the fish will prefer one type of surface lure/fly, sometimes they will hit anything, and sometimes merely switching from one lure/fly to another is enough to trigger a strike.

Grass Beds, Buzzbaits, and Cork Poppers

One of the most memorable mossybacks of my fishing career was a fish that followed a ¼-inch buzzbait for over 15 yards, hitting and missing it three times before finally hooking itself on the fourth assault. After such vigorous pursuit, I was expecting the smallmouth of a lifetime, or at least a fish that flirted with the four-pound mark—a hefty stream smallie anywhere in America. Instead, the fish barely topped a pound and only measured 14 inches.

Buzzbaits do seem to rev up river bass like no other lure, and I have caught smallmouths of over 20 inches that came charging after these churning blade baits. And the most likely place to prospect for smallies with this lure is some sort of vegetation. This vegetation can be above the water line, such as water willow, which often flourishes on islets. Or it can be vegetation that flourishes beneath the surface, such as elodea, star grass, or curly leaf pondweed.

For above-the-water vegetation, cast your buzzer parallel to the weed bed, especially the downstream side. For the latter, run the lure across the vegetation, particularly if rock or wood cover exists nearby.

Obviously, no fly rod pattern can come close to duplicating the noise that a buzzbait can. Nevertheless, fly fishermen have a nifty noise option, believes Brit Stoudenmire, who operates Canoe the New Outfitters in Pearisburg, Virginia.

"A big Cork Popper makes more racket when it lands than any other fly pattern that I have used," said Stoudenmire. "It's a great choice when you are fishing a grass bed, especially under low light conditions. When that popper lands, it will send out waves over long distances. Don't even think about moving that popper until all the waves and even dimples have died down and you've counted to ten or so. Give the popper time to 'call' to the bass."

Insider Tips

Don't believe that because brown bass have "small mouths," you have to employ small lures like ⅛-ounce buzzbaits. I never tie on a buzzbait smaller than ¼-ounce, and a ⅜-ounce model can force some jarring strikes from trophy mossybacks. My favorite buzzbait is a ¼-ounce Hart Stopper. Skirt color is irrelevant because this is purely a reaction bait.

Similarly, don't opt for size 6 or 8 Cork Poppers, emphasizes Stoudenmire. He prefers size 2 models because of the "big splat" caused by the large cork body.

The Main Channel, Crankbaits, and Clousers

Mike Smith, who operates Greasy Creek Outfitters in Willis, Virginia, guides on the New River, a stream famous—or infamous—for having smallmouths holding well off the bank in deep water, especially along main channel drop-offs.

"I often use crankbaits during the warm weather period, especially if we have high, turbid water, and Clouser Minnows if we don't," said Smith. "Generally speaking, I have a rod set up with 8-pound test when the water is high. I especially like chartreuse or fire tiger colors and a medium-deep running bait so that I can work the mid-river ledges and chunk rock that are at least 10 to 20 feet off the bank and in or near the main channel. A white Clouser Minnow can be worked in stops and starts over this same habitat and can bring the same reaction strikes."

Smith says that the main channel/crankbait and Clouser pattern will work well during the spring and pre-spawn periods when the water rises and the smallmouths temporarily move off the banks to the deeper areas just offshore where the current isn't as taxing and where they can hold in depths of more than six feet. But the guide adds that after the spawn period and throughout most of the rest of the warm water period, good-sized smallmouths will again relate to the main channel, especially if they can make use of current breaks behind submerged mid-river boulders.

"We have caught some real 'chunks' using this pattern," concluded the guide.

Crankbait Choices

- "My favorite crankbait by far is the Bomber Model A, sizes 6 through 8," said Smith.

- Other good choices: Cordell Big O, Bandit 200 and 300 series, Bill Lewis Rat-L-Traps, Storm Wiggle Warts, Rapala Fat Raps, Yo-Zuri Hardcore Crankbaits.

- Besides the Clouser, other minnow patterns include the CK Baitfish, Trow's Minnow, and the Muddler Minnow.

Insider Tips

"I like Izorline Platinum Copolymer Mono and Spiderwire Super Mono XXX for everything, but especially crankbaits and jerkbaits because these lines are low stretch, low memory, abrasive resistant, and invisible in the water," said Smith. "All are good qualities for river fishing. I never use braided line, even for plastics, on the river."

For guided trips with Mike Smith, contact him at (540) 789-7811 or www.greasycreekoutfitters.com.

Eddies and Runs, Grubs, and Gummy Minnows

Virginia guide Ron Evans maintains that grubs are among the most versatile of river baits, especially when worked through eddies, runs, and other moving water situations.

"You can swim a grub to imitate a baitfish, or you can crawl one on the river bottom to imitate a crawdad or a hellgrammite," he said. "I really like to fish grubs in faster current by swimming them through medium depth cobblestone areas to draw out the more active smallies, or throw them into eddies to entice fish that might not be as active."

Evans relates that an important attribute of grubs is their ease of use. Beginners as well as experts can quickly learn to swim a grub, which is merely retrieving this bait back with the current. Grubs will attract smallmouths of all sizes, but Evans also notes that last year, two of his 12 smallmouths that went 20 inches or more fell to grubs.

For guided trips with Ron Evans, contact him at Riverbound Guide Service at (703) 753-5533 or riverbound29@yahoo.com.

One of the best fly patterns of any kind that I have seen is the Gummy Minnow, created by Roanoke Virginia guide and fly shop operator, Blane Chocklett. The Gummy has the look and feel of soft plastic, yet it is undeniably a fly pattern and in the water, looks just like a darting, fleeing minnow or dace. This is an ideal choice for probing eddies, runs, and, for that matter, swift water of any kind. For more information, contact Chocklett at Blue Ridge Fly Fishers at (540) 563-1617 or www.blueridgeflyfishers.com.

Good Grubs
- 3-inch Berkley Powerbait, Cabela's Action Tail, Mister Twister Curly Tail Grub, Kalin's Salty Lunker.

For bigger smallmouths, Ron Evans recommends river anglers use 4- to 5-inch models; his favorites are grubs made by Kalin's, Zoom, and Case Plastics. Rig one on a Charlie Brewer slider head. Try natural colors, continued Evans, in clear water but switch to chartreuse or black for stained conditions.

Chapter 13

$\mathcal{S}$urface Flies and Lures

Come the dog days, America's best largemouth lakes often become very difficult to fish because of the heat, pleasure boat traffic, and heavily pressured fish. An alternative to visiting these impoundments is for anglers to venture to this country's smallmouth rivers and streams where the action is often at its peak. What's more, the best patterns for the mid- to late summer period often involve the use of surface lures and flies. Here are five great patterns for this summer.

The Early Morning/Late Evening Cruising the Shallows Pattern

Several summers ago, a friend and I launched our canoe just before dawn on Virginia's James River. Having taken that particular trip many times, I knew that a water willow bed lies directly across the stream from the access point. Paddling within casting distance of the vegetation, I tossed a soft plastic jerkbait into the less than a foot deep liquid that borders the bed. Almost immediately, my line went taut, and seconds later I set the hook into what later proved to be a four-pound smallmouth that I was able to land and release.

The early morning/late evening cruising-the-shallows pattern is certainly one of the most reliable—although briefest—on our best smallmouth rivers. At these two times of the day, look for the bass to be near various kinds of cover but not holding on them. For example, the aforementioned water willow bed extends for some 20 yards, and the jumbo brown bass I caught from it spit up a crayfish and several minnows as I was releasing it. The smallie was likely going up and down the sides of the vegetation, feeding indiscriminately on a minnow or two here, a crayfish or a hellgrammite there and if the bass were really lucky, perhaps even a frog.

Smallmouths instinctively know that this brief period of low light is a time of great activity for the various creatures that live along the shallow edges between water and land. The fish are in a hurry to cover as much edge as possible before the rising or setting sun changes the conditions— and the activity levels of their prey.

For this shallow water situation, use flies and baits that can be thrown long distances, such as weighted nymphs and soft plastic jerkbaits, and that create little disturbance when they land. And when this thin water bite is over, don't waste time thinking that you can extend it— go on to the next pattern.

The Current Break Pattern of Early to Midmorning

And that next pattern is often the early to midmorning current break one. Jeff Kelble, who operates Fishing in Virginia, favors a size 2 cup faced popper for topwater action around wood and rock current breaks.

"A reminder, though, presentation becomes critical during low clear water conditions," said the guide. "Generally, I'm going to set the boat about 25 feet or so cross current from the edge of the break and work the near seam first. Then I'll move the boat in some so that I can work deeper into the protected water behind the obstruction. If the current break is large enough, I'll actually row into it to fish the far seam and the tail-out of the pocket when appropriate.

"It often helps to cast so that a little of the fly line crosses the current edge into the slow water behind the obstruction. That little bit of line acts like an anchor and allows you to manipulate line to work your fly how you like, that is, to slow your fly enough so that you control the presentation."

For guided trips with Kelble, contact him at The Boyce Bed and Breakfast at (540) 837-1478, www.potomacriverkeeper.org (Web site), or jeff@shenandoahriverkeeper.org (e-mail).

When employing a spinning rod to work a current break, I practice none of the subtlety that Kelble does with a long rod. My go-to lure is a ¼-ounce buzzbait, and I want it to be churning through the pocket water at a rapid pace. After two quick casts with the buzzer—with the goal being to pick off an actively feeding smallmouth—I then turn to chuggers, poppers and/or hard and soft plastic stick baits.

The Shoreline-Shade Pattern of High Noon

On American impoundments, the hour before and after high noon is a period of extremely poor fishing as the increasing heat, thrashing swimmers, and churning jet boats send the bass deep. On our rivers, however, high noon brings some of the best and most predictable bassing of the day.

That is because river and stream smallmouths typically move to the banks then and stack up in certain places, specifically where the shoreline canopy creates small shady sanctuaries around downed trees, brush piles, or underwater boulders and rock piles. My basic premise is that as my canoe cruises down a bank, every tenth or so submerged tree, brush pile, or rock will hold a nice bronzeback.

For example, this past summer two friends and I were floating West Virginia's New River during the noontime period. I proclaimed that it would be impossible for the three of us—as we probed a shade speckled shoreline that extended for about a mile—to make more than 15 casts without hooking a two-pound or larger mossback. For over an hour we fished the shoreline—and no one went more than 12 casts without a hookup.

The Match-the-Hatch Pattern of Early and Mid-Afternoon

Britt Stoudenmire, who operates Canoe the New Outfitters—www.icanoethenew.com—in Pearisburg, Virginia, relishes the match the hatch pattern of early and mid-afternoon.

"Smallmouth bass fishing is unlike trout fishing in the fact that on many rivers, flies are not an essential part of a smallmouth's diet, especially during the summer months when crawfish, hellgrammites, and baitfish are so readily available," explained Stoudenmire. "What is important, though, about a hatch is that a strong one can start a chain reaction that inevitably triggers a feeding spurt by the largest bass. And when bass become aggressive like that, they—unlike trout—will take advantage of just about any opportunity to feed on whatever comes by."

Stoudenmire says that on the New River, caddis, damsel, or dragonfly hatches are the ones most likely to initiate an early to mid-afternoon feeding spree by the smallmouths. Obviously, long rodders can choose to match the hatch with patterns that mimic these creatures. But both fly and spin fishermen should not be concerned whether their flies or lures accurately imitate what the smallmouths are feeding on. As the outfitter noted earlier, when larger river smallmouths begin to feed, they often are not particular about what a bait or fly looks like.

Insider Tips

On our rivers, damsel and dragonfly hatches typically occur in mid-river regions, often far away from any recognizable cover or structure. Also, expect the sub 12-inch bass to turn on first, as they gulp down damsels in distress, often leaping from the water as they do so. Later, expect the big sow smallies to join the fray. But don't expect these larger bass to make spectacles of themselves and betray their presence as they will not be leaping about like their smaller brethren. The bigger bass will more likely be foraging just under the surface on the sunfish, chubs, and minnows that are attracted to the various hatches.

The Jitterbug and Big Blockhead Pattern at Sunset

For generations, rural youths have ambled down to farm ponds at dusk and worked Arbogast Jitterbugs across the surface. The gentle side-to-side swaying of this lure has been the downfall of many a pond largemouth.

Jitterbugs have the ability to bewitch river brown bass as well at this time of day. Several areas especially can produce solid numbers of fish, but my favorite has to be a downed tree that lies perpendicular to the

Surface flies and lures can produce scintillating summertime stream action.

shoreline. Let the jitterbug do its seductive wobble along the entire length of the tree and, what's more, maintain that retrieve all the way to the boat. In this situation, a smallmouth is just as likely to hit a Jitterbug at the start of the retrieve as it is when the lure nears a craft.

Another good place to work a Jitterbug at dusk is a rocky pool in four to eight feet of water, particularly if this pool borders a rapid or riffle. Also check out expansive eddies replete with chunk rock.

Don't work a Jitterbug through swiftly moving water as the pace of the current negates the attractive qualities of this lure. Do maintain the steady pace of the retrieve even if a smallmouth misses this lure several times. I have had smallies hit a Jitterbug three or four times before actually hooking them.

Noted stream smallmouth fly fishing expert Tim Holschlag once showed me how to use his surface creation, the Big Blockhead in a way that, though not reminiscent of a jitterbug, had the same bewitching effect on stream smallmouths. To explain, a jitterbug wobbles across the water like a frog swimming unconcernedly along. In contrast, Holschlag gives short, quick snaps to the Blockhead, making it look like a frog that is trying to jump from the water and escape from a pursuing predator. As is true with the jitterbug, the Blockhead performs best in still water, losing its hypnotic effect in current. For more information, visit Holschlag's Web site www.smallmouthangler.com.

Must Have Topwater Lure Categories

Seven categories of baits qualify as must-have lures for river smallmouth fanatics:

- Prop baits: Heddon Tiny Torpedo, Bill Lewis Rat-L-Top, Phillips Crippled Killer, Rapala Skitter Prop.

- Chuggers: Rebel Pop-R, Berkley Frenzy Popper, Cabela's Fisherman Series Top Popper, Rapala Skitter Pop.

- Stick Baits: Heddon Zara Spook, Storm Chug Bug, Lucky Craft Sammy, Berkley Frenzy Walker.

- Hard Plastic Floating Minnow baits: Cabela's Livin' Minnow, Cordell Red Fin, Rebel Minnow, Rapala Original, Yo-Zuri Crystal Minnow.

- Wobblers: Arbogast Jitterbug, Cabela's Fisherman Series June Frog

- Soft Plastic Jerkbaits: Almost every soft plastic bait company has an entry.

- Buzzbaits: My personal favorite is the Hart Stopper ¼-ounce buzzer. For bigger smallmouths, guide Mike Smith, (www.greasycreekoutfitters.com) uses buzzers in the ⅜-ounce size.

Topwater fly patterns for the long rodder:

- For summertime fly patterns, Kevin Howell, who operates Davidson River Outfitters (www.davidsonflyfishing.com), lists these as his favorites: Chocklett's Disc Slider in chartreuse, Sneaky Pete in chartreuse, Dink in purple or chartreuse, and Clouser's Floating Minnow.

- My favorites include the Sneaky Pete Popper, the Big Blockhead, Walt's Poppers, Grasshopper Patterns, Cup-faced Poppers, and Blane Chocklett's Damsel and Dragonflies.

Chapter 14

*S*ummertime Smallmouths:
Topwater Time All Day Long

"You see it, don't you?" As he spoke, Britt Stoudenmire nodded toward the rapidly approaching eddy. It loomed on river right just past a railroad trestle, and this area of reversing currents lay partially in shade and partially out—thanks to shadows coming from the bridge and a sycamore-shrouded bank. Adding to the appeal were the boulders that pocked the eddy.

I nodded back to Britt, who along with his wife, Leigh, operates Canoe the New Outfitters and Guide Service in Pearisburg, Virginia, and cocked my medium action spinning rod. On the business end of the 10-pound test was a No. 11 Rapala Original Floater minnow. Britt then used his right oar to ease his raft closer to the eddy.

"You want first crack, don't you?" grinned fellow guide Marty Shaffner.

My response was to sidearm the Rapala into the heart of the eddy, feathering the lure downward at the end of the cast so that it lightly landed. The hard plastic jerkbait had barely dimpled the surface when a smallmouth reared up from the depths and savaged the bogus minnow.

"Get away from the rocks," I yelled, fearing that the first action of the smallmouth would be to charge back toward the eddy's bottom and its boulders.

But Britt had already anticipated the bronzeback's reaction and had expertly maneuvered his craft into the deeper water of the main channel. A minute or so later, I landed, then released, the two-pounder.

I keep detailed records of every fishing trip and every bass I catch that measures 12 inches or better. My records show that that smallie was caught on July 19 at 1:40 p.m., not exactly prime fishing or topwater time

The Rapala Original Floater

One of the best topwater baits of all time is the same as the best selling artificial of all time—the Rapala Original Floater. Invented by Finnish lure designer Lauri Rapala, this minnow plug made its way to America in 1960. But its big break came in August of 1962 when *Life* magazine ran an article on the Rapala in the same issue that carried a major feature on the death of Marilyn Monroe.

"The heyday for sales of the Rapala Original Floater came in the 1960s and 1970s with the article in *Life* coinciding with the Monroe story really giving the lure fantastic exposure," said David James, field promotions manager for Normark. "But the Original started to fall out of popularity in the 1980s when we came out with the Shad Rap."

The truth is, however, that the Rapala Original has never stopped being an exceptionally effective lure for surface feeding smallmouths. Ironically, James says that most anglers who buy the lure today are after walleyes, although there is a hardcore group of bass fishermen that still rely on it.

"You can finesse the Original by slowly walking it across the surface, jerking it across the top, or cranking it down," said James. "No matter how you fish the Original, the bait still catches fish like it always has because of the realistic action."

anywhere in the country—that is, unless you're afloat on one of America's smallmouth rivers.

Many anglers avoid fishing largemouth-filled lakes during the heat of the dog days, and at that time they especially relegate topwater baits to the hinterlands of tackle boxes. But in the moving water of our rivers, smallmouths typically feed aggressively on top throughout much of a summer day. In fact, Stoudenmire believes that surface lures and fly patterns are among the best choices then.

"Many fishermen use topwater lures and flies during the summer because they like to see the smallmouths hit on the surface, but these

Rod, Reel, and Line Lineup

For buzzbaits: Loomis IMX 6-foot medium heavy baitcasting rod (CR723) with a Quantum Energy PT baitcasting reel spooled with Power Pro 20/6 braided line. "I like the fast action, medium heavy rod and braided line for quick, stout hooksets and for moving big fish away from cover," said Stoudenmire. "I like the Quantum baitcasting reel for its high 6.3:1 gear ratio to get the buzzer up quickly and keep it moving in currents."

For all other topwater baits: Loomis GLX 6-foot medium spinning rod (SJR722) with a Shimano Symetre 2500 spinning reel spooled with Power Pro 20/6 braided line. "The medium action of the GLX rods imparts a nice action on the baits and aids in landing big fish on topwater baits with treble hooks," explained the guide.

fishermen don't stop to analyze why, when, and where the bass are hitting on topwater," he says. "I believe that prop and chugger baits, and of course buzzbaits, as well as fly rod poppers and hair bugs, are good all-day warm weather lures and fly patterns, and I will throw them all day.

"What I will change is where I fish, alternating between mid-river current breaks, runs and riffles, and shade pockets along the banks, depending on the time of day and the sun factor."

The buzzbait/popper bite is an especially powerful one during the summertime. For example, both Stoudenmire and Shaffner cast good-sized buzzbaits and poppers throughout our outing from the time we put in at 11:15 a.m. until we left the New at dark. The best mossybacks for both the guides were ones that measured just under 20 inches.

Marty's lunker came around 2 p.m. in the heat of the day as he was retrieving the blade bait through a current break formed by a boulder within an outside bend. And Britt's prize was one that was holding in a deep-water run and waylaid a buzzer as the sun set. These anecdotes lead to several important points about summertime topwater fishing on rivers.

First, as noted earlier, the topwater bite does endure all day. Good-sized smallies, like Shaffner's fish, often move into feeding lanes behind current obstructions, and they hold there both in the heat of the day and

Summertime river smallmouths will often strike topwater flies
and lures throughout the day.

during low light conditions. The key to this sustained activity is the fact
that the river's current—and the well-oxygenated water that results—
ensures that activity levels of smallmouths and their prey species will be
high throughout the day.

Second, anglers should definitely not follow the conventional wisdom
that their "small mouths" require us to downsize our lures or flies.
Stoudenmire's nearly four-pound smallmouth fell for a ³⁄₈-ounce

For fishing topwater flies:

○ A 9-foot, 8-weight Loomis GLX (FR1088) with a Ross Rhythm 3.5 fly-reel spooled with a Wulff bass taper 8-weight floating fly line.

○ Frog Hair 7-foot, 10-pound (11 pound tensile strength) tapered bass leader and 10-to-12-pound-test tippet when necessary.

○ "I like the 8-weight rod for casting the bigger flies more effectively, increased efficiency on hooksets, and moving big fish out of dense cover," said Britt.

buzzbait—a size that is common in the tackle boxes of lake largemouth fishermen. For some strange reason, many river runners feel that they have to tie on ⅛-ounce buzzers. Occasionally, of course, these anglers will catch good-sized fish. But too much of their time is spent (wasted) removing from their hooks the hordes of eight-inch fish that blow up on tiny buzzbaits.

Fly fishermen share this misbegotten small fly hang up with their spin fishermen brethren. Tie on a size 4 Hopper instead of a size 8 or 10. Live dangerously and catch fewer but bigger stream smallmouths.

Third, as Stoudenmire mentioned earlier, the "sun factor" is an important consideration. For instance, Marty's fish was holding behind a boulder not only because it serves as a current break but also because shade had extended outward from the trees that grow along the outside bend.

Throughout the day, even during the midday hours when the sun is directly overhead, shade pockets will exist on a river. Sometimes these pockets will only be little slivers of shadows along the shoreline. Nevertheless, smallies will seek out these areas if current, structure, and/or cover exist. Stoudenmire urges anglers to find these shadowy locales and diligently work topwater baits and flies through them. And buzzbaits and grasshopper patterns are not the only lures and flies that will bring results.

"Popping and chugger-style baits can also be excellent topwater presentations for attracting these fish," revealed Britt. "I like to cast to the shady banks, make one or two slight pops, and then let the popper drift for about five seconds before repeating the presentation.

"These baits are very versatile and can be worked fast or slow depending on the current conditions and mood of the fish."

Other Major Patterns

When the water becomes overly low and clear, Stoudenmire turns to walk-the-dog-style twitch baits.

"These baits produce a more subtle spitting, walking, splashing action, and can be worked in a variety of ways to attract lethargic and spooky fish," said Stoudenmire. "Walk-the-dog-style baits are excellent choices for targeting feeding smallmouths holding in shallow riffle drop-offs directly adjacent to grass beds. Many times, these fish use the slight drop-offs and riffles as cover as they wait to ambush their prey moving in and out of the grass beds."

Interestingly, Stoudenmire notes that lures are not always the best choices for surface feeding smallies.

"If there is one time of year that topwater flies completely out-fish lures, it would be the dog days of summer in August," he offered. "When the water is extremely low, clear, and hot, the subtle presentation of a deer hair bug or popper hitting the surface during a midday hatch can be absolutely deadly in attracting large smallmouth that seem reluctant to hit anything else."

Another excellent long rod pattern, continues Stoudenmire, involves working sliders and divers around current breaks either near the banks or

Stoudenmire's Lure and Fly Favorites

Lures: ⅜-ounce Butch Neal buzzbait, Excalibur Spit'n Image, Lucky Craft Sammy, Rebel Pop-R, Zara Spooks, Case Sinkin' Salty Shads and Minnows.

Fly Patterns: Walt Holman Super Slider, Dahlberg Diver, Cup Face, and Block Poppers, and Deer Hair bugs.

behind mid-river boulders and ledges. These patterns perform better than poppers and deer hair bugs because they possess "a slight diving action as they swing out of the pockets."

Topwater action can be excellent on our country's premier smallmouth rivers throughout the course of a day and the summer itself. Find the current and right kind of structure and cover and use Britt Stoudenmire's tackle, lure, and fly tips, and you should be all set.

Britt Stoudenmire Biography

Britt and Leigh Stoudenmire opened Canoe the New Outfitters & Guide Service in the spring of 2004. A graduate of Virginia Tech and the Citadel as well as a former college baseball pitcher, Britt is an avid outdoor enthusiast and has hunted and fished his entire life. Spending over 200 days a year on both the New and James rivers guiding and fishing, Britt is respected as one of the most knowledgeable and hard working smallmouth guides in Southwest Virginia. He is on the Pro-Staff for G. Loomis rods, Ross Reels, and Wulff Fly Lines.

Britt focuses the majority of his trips on targeting mature (18 inches or bigger) smallmouth bass on both spin and fly gear and teaching his clients the techniques needed to effectively pursue these fish. During the past three years, Britt's clients have caught and released over 100 Virginia citation smallmouths (20 inches or longer). For more information, call (540) 921-7438 or go to www.icanoethenew.com.

For more information on guided trips with Marty Shaffner, contact him at (336) 957-4630, (336) 902-0044, or www.tristateangler.com.

Chapter 15

Debunking the Myths about Topwaters

Not long ago, I gave a bass fishing seminar, and during the question and answer period, I responded to more questions about topwater baits than any other lure category. As a group, audience members held the following misconceptions about surface artificials and flies, "myths" that too many anglers seem to cling to:

- They regard topwaters as just being summer lures and flies.
- They consider topwaters just morning and evening baits.
- They go with just two or three favorites, refusing to experiment with different ones. And if they do experiment, they try a new lure or fly for only a few casts before going back to their favorites.
- They pay too little attention to matching rods and line with their surface offerings.
- They believe that the number one reason to employ topwaters is to see bass hit a bait on the surface.

Let's debunk these fallacies one by one.

Myth 1: Topwaters are Just Summertime Lures

Granted, artificial lures and flies work great during June, July, and August, but depending on where you live in this country, topwater action can occur as soon as mid-March and as late as mid-November. The key is water temperature, not calendar date.

This point was hammered home to me several years ago. My best fishing buddy and I were visiting our favorite fishing hole on a late April Saturday. The temperatures that spring had been "normal," or as normal

Topwater Trends

A current trend concerning the creation of new topwater baits is to take a tried and true design and alter it slightly. For example, one of my hottest surface baits is a chugger: the Rapala Skitter Pop, which was introduced in the late 1990s. Mark Fisher, director of field promotions for Rapala, says the company's next logical step was to make some design changes to the Skitter Pop and come up with a prop bait: the Skitter Prop.

The Skitter Prop, says Fisher, fulfills an entirely new and separate niche from the Skitter Pop. This same trend can be seen with the Heddon Wounded Spook. This is a 4½-inch front/rear prop bait that engenders a great deal of noise. The Wounded Spook is, of course, an offshoot of the famous walk-the-dog cigar bait: the Zara Spook.

This same trend can be seen in soft plastic topwaters such as jerkbaits. Once the original Lunker City Slug-Go made an appearance, Lunker City and other companies have fiddled with the body shape, tail construction, and overall size of the jerkbaits to create whole new looks and topwater applications.

as spring temperatures ever are. So my friend and I went out that morning armed with our standard spring baits and flies: streamers, nymphs, spinnerbaits, crankbaits, and jig and pigs. We caught a few bass, but arrived back at the ramp with the sense that we should have done much better.

At the ramp, my companion and I ran into an acquaintance that seemed beside himself with smug satisfaction. He regaled us with his "epic day," enthusing that the bass had hit surface offerings all day long. The water temperature that day: 58 degrees.

The lesson here is that once the water temperature rises to or remains in the mid-50s—regardless of month or season—topwater baits and flies should be tried. This is especially true if a warming trend has recently occurred.

Myth 2: Topwaters are Just Morning and Evening Baits

Obviously, low light conditions remain prime times to churn a buzzbait, walk a Zara Spook, spit pop a Rebel Pop-R, slurp about a Storm Chug Bug, bloop a Big Blockhead, and snap a Sneaky Peter. But more and more, especially in the summer months, my best topwater action takes place in the heat of the midday period.

I first realized this tendency a number of years ago. A friend had wanted me to show him how to work the Arbogast Jitterbug—a classic topwater that rarely makes appearances in modern day tackle boxes. We maneuvered our boat over to a shaded shoreline where, for demonstration purposes only, I began returning the Jitterbug in the "high riding" side-to-side motion it is known for. A four-pounder intercepted the retrieve, and another hefty bass soon repeated the same mistake as its predecessor. Since that day, when the air temperature rises and the shoreline canopy creates a shady sanctuary, I allow the Jitterbug to do its little dance.

A second superlative midday choice is a Sneaky Peter Popper. On a hot summer day in the 1980s, I first saw how effective the Sneaky Pete is during the midday period. A friend instructed me to toss the Sneaky Pete into the shade pockets below sycamores.

"What do I do next?" I asked.

"Nothing," he replied. "Except maybe you either look away or close your eyes. Just leave the Pete in place."

Amazingly, I had smallmouths popping the Pete as soon as 90 seconds after I had cast it, even though I had not given the pattern any movement since it splashed down.

Another marvelous midday topwater is a buzzbait. Any time I encounter aquatic vegetation, a postage stamp size smattering of shade, current near cover of any kind, I will toss a ¼- or ⅜-ounce Hart Stopper Buzzbait or a ³⁄₁₆-ounce Strike King Tri-Wing Buzz King.

I have talked to a few anglers who do toss topwaters in the midday hours, but they tend to adhere to what I call a "myth within a myth," believing that surface baits, if used at all under a high sun, should be left motionless for long periods of time. Midday bass are "extremely sluggish" goes the old saw. Actually, I have had my best success with poppers, chuggers, and stick baits while violently retrieving them across the surface...the Sneaky Pete being the exception.

The lesson from all this is that we should let the bass tell us when and how they want topwater baits and flies presented. We should not let the conventional wisdom box us in to a certain line of thinking.

Myth 3: Stick to Your Favorite Topwaters

Nearly everyone, this writer included, has preferred topwater baits and flies they feel can produce bass during adverse conditions. Many anglers, however, rely on just two or three favorite topwaters, which greatly restricts them from being able to adapt to new or emerging conditions on a body of water.

For example, suppose you are an expert with chugger-style baits and flies. You have been able to catch several nice bass on a chugger while slowly motoring past downed timber along a 100-yard-long outside bend. You make another pass down this shoreline while still employing the chugger. This time, though, your lure or fly is ignored.

A better gambit for the second pass would have been to switch to another category of topwater—a Zara spook-style lure or Big Blockhead, a hair bug or slim minnow, or a soft plastic jerkbait or Chocklett Damselfly—and give the bass an entirely different look. And anglers often cannot give the fish this different look unless they have mastered, or at least become competent in, a wide variety of topwaters.

For instance, one of my hard plastic topwater tackle boxes contains a quartet of propeller baits: two Heddon Tiny Torpedoes (in baby bass and frog), a Bill Lewis Rat-L-Top, and a Phillips Crippled Killer. All these lures either offer a different color (in the case of the Torpedoes) or a different sound. The Crippled Killer seems to be the most aggressive noise maker of the lures while the Rat-L-Top seems to be the least intrusive with the two Torpedoes somewhere in between. My point is that even lures within the same category of baits can create considerably different sounds.

And if the prop baits don't produce, I often opt for chuggers such as a Rebel Pop-R, Pradco's Pop-N-Image or Rapala Skitter Pop. They too create quite different sounds. Other very different options in my hard plastic tackle box include walk-the-dog baits like the Zara Spook or Storm Chug Bug, minnow lures like a Cordell Red Fin or Rapala Original Minnow, and, of course, buzzbaits.

Fly fishermen should have the same array of options. For instance, years ago, I purchased a box of fly patterns, all of them different. Included were poppers, chuggers, sliders, grasshoppers, and crickets, among others. Experiment with retrieves, patterns, and locations until something works—or you arrive at the take-out point.

Soft plastic topwaters can also be tossed into the mix. Jerkbaits, floating worms and frogs, and wacky-rigged worms are other possibilities. The lesson here is to change bait categories, retrieves, and even colors until you have truly exploited the topwater bite in an area. Plus, this year, promise yourself to become reasonably adept with a topwater new to the market or at least a category of surface bait or fly that you had been previously unfamiliar with.

Myth 4: Use Your Regular Rod and Line for Topwaters

Jim Ayres operates Gone Fishin' in Oak Hill, West Virginia, a guide service that takes clients on three major kinds of waters: lowland lakes, highland reservoirs, and upland rivers. He is frequently amazed at his clients' lack of knowledge concerning the need to balance their equipment for topwater angling.

"I often have to tell my clients what type of rods and reels to bring," he said. "For topwaters, too many people believe just any old rod or line will do, and that's not true. Many people like to use a light action rod because they want to 'play' a fish. But a light action outfit results in you having too slow a reaction time on the hookset and not enough power to give you a good hookset.

"Other fishermen go to the opposite extreme. They want to use a heavy action rod so they can slug it out with a bass. But that outfit results

Blane Chocklett, who operates Blue Ridge Fly Fishers in Roanoke, Virginia, is an expert at fooling big river smallmouths with a fly.

in you having too fast a reaction time and will even pull a bait away from a bass. The best compromise is a medium heavy spinning rod."

Ayres prefers a 6 ½-foot Berkley Lightning Spinning Rod and 8-pound-test Ande line in low visibility green. Seven-foot rods offer great casting distance, but they slap the water too much when a topwater is being retrieved. Six-foot rods don't enable surface baits to be cast as far as is often required. Spinning rods, the guide continues, are selected because they are better than baitcasters for retrieving 8-pound test.

"Now, some people may question my choice of 8-pound test," said Ayres. "But this weight line enables a surface lure to move much more naturally than 10- or 12-pound test does, for example. Also, you really don't need heavier line for topwaters. The only reason to use heavy line is to get a bass up and out of cover when you are using subsurface baits. With topwaters, a bass has already left cover to hit your lure."

Classic Topwaters

What makes a topwater lure become a classic? Bruce Staunton, former director of public relations for Pradco, offered a potential answer.

"I think a classic topwater lure would be a bait that has a design that no one else has thought of, that consistently catches fish, and that has consistently stood the test of time," he said. "For example, Pradco has at least two baits that I would consider classics: the Zara Spook, created by James Heddon; and the Jitterbug, created by Fred Arbogast. In the case of the Jitterbug, who would have thought that a broomstick handle and two spoons melted down would have evolved into a classic bait."

Certainly another classic topwater is the Rapala Original Minnow, created in 1936 by Lauri Rapala. Rapala's Mark Fisher had a simple answer to the question why the Rapala is considered a topwater standard: "That lure makes people better anglers."

The lesson here, of course, is that matching your rod, reel, and line for the topwaters you use really does matter. For guided trips with Jim Ayres, call (888) 470-3131.

Fly fishermen often make similar mistakes. For example, a good friend of mine and I decided to go fly fishing with topwater patterns on a creek tributary of the James. My buddy, saying it would be "fun" to use a light rod, showed up with a 4-weight rod that would have been ideal for fishing for native brook trout. However, our goal that day was to target keeper-sized bronzebacks. My buddy was hopelessly mismatched and he was unable to land a single decent smallmouth.

Another reason not to use inadequate fly rods is that playing a nice smallie on a light fly rod (or spinning outfit) is very stressful to the fish themselves. Most anglers, myself included, release all the smallmouths they catch. If we are to do so and if the fish are to have a reasonable chance of surviving afterward, we owe it to them to land and release them quickly, so that the stress does not cause inordinate amounts of lactic acid to build up in their systems (which can cause death).

Myth 5: Use Topwaters Because They're Fun Baits

Of course, many of us find it festive to see a bass submarine to the surface and smash a topwater bait or fly. And I have had many anglers tell me their number one reason to employ a topwater is that they like to see the proverbial "wash basin-sized boils" that a big surface-feeding bass creates. But, really, that should be the last reason to tie on a surface pattern. The best reason to tie on any fly or lure is because it is the logical choice to catch fish at that particular time.

Topwater baits and flies are angling tools just like any category of lure is. Certain tools—and certain lure/fly kinds—perform better at certain times. The lesson here is that there's nothing wrong with having fun when fishing, of course, but the best kind of fun is catching quality bass.

Myths and misconceptions, fallacies and fiction, lunacies and legends—topwater baits and flies probably have had more untrue beliefs assigned to them than any other category. Dispel your preconceived notions about topwaters and see your bass fishing improve.

Chapter 16

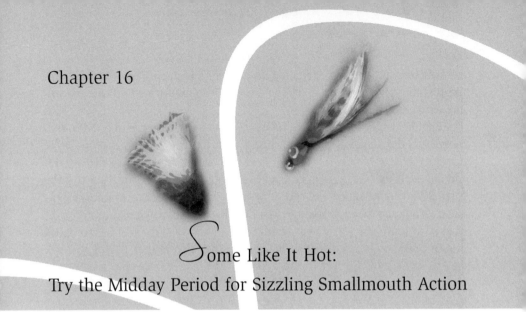

$\mathcal{S}$ome Like It Hot:
Try the Midday Period for Sizzling Smallmouth Action

A growing number of hardcore river smallmouth anglers have discovered that they really like the hottest time of day during the hottest time of the year. For when the blistering summer sun hammers the nation's premier smallmouth rivers, it is then that the day's best action often takes place.

By far, my favorite kind of fishing is plying upland rivers for bronzebacks. Over the years, all my summertime 4-pound-plus mossbacks (the 4-pound mark is the gold standard for trophy river smallmouths across the country) except one have been caught between 11 a.m. and 4 p.m. Dave Arnold, who operates Class VI River Runners in Lansing, West Virginia—(800) 252-7784—agrees about this time period's magic.

"If we have a client who is serious about catching big smallmouths on the New River, many times we don't even put a raft on the river until around noon," he said. "I know a lot of people are conditioned to getting up early and going fishing in the summertime, especially if they are traveling to an impoundment. But the lake setting is so much different from that of a river. The boating traffic and the still water alone are enough to make the midday bite slow. The moving water environment of a smallmouth river makes the fish more active in the summer anyway. And then there is the hatch factor."

The hatch factor that Arnold refers to involves the many aquatic insects that begin to emerge, reproduce, or become active in the early afternoon. Two of the most anticipated hatches of any summer day are the damselfly and dragonfly ones. Many times I have endured a slow period of fishing until this insect duo begins to do their thing. Sometimes masses of newly adult damselflies and dragonflies will congregate on aquatic vegetation such as water willow; other times, these winged predators will hover over the water in search of their quarry; some days, they will helicopter about as they lay eggs.

The important point to remember is that when the warmth of midday sends damsels and dragons into action, the activity level of the smallmouths is also jumpstarted. Add in the hatches of mayfly, caddis, stoneflies, and a host of other creatures—schools of minnows and sunfish are subsequently turned on as well—and it is easy to understand why a mossyback river becomes a maelstrom of activity when Old Sol hangs high.

Midday Topwater Baits and Flies

How can we take advantage of this midday topwater activity? Long rodders obviously turn to patterns that imitate damsel and dragonflies, and I have experienced success with these flies. Thankfully, though, black bass are not as prey specific as trout are. When a stream smallie is looking upward, it is not prone to gently sipping in minute creatures like a salmonid is. Instead, smallmouths take on the aggressive mode of an NFL defensive end who is about to blindside a quarterback.

For example, one summer several friends and I were fishing the James River near my Southwest Virginia home. Predictably, the morning bite had been uninspiring, but around 1 p.m. we noticed bank swallows skimming over the water feeding on insects and, as we paddled closer, large swirls occurring on the surface.

I tossed a 3½-inch Rapala Skitter Prop in a frog pattern into the hubbub and a 2½-pound smallmouth ceased dining on tiny insects and instead adopted a steak-and-potato diet. Before we finished working the area, my group had dueled with a number of bass in the 2- to 3-pound range. Several lessons can be learned from this anecdote.

First, just as is often true on impoundments, larger topwater lures and flies catch larger river smallmouths. I am always amazed at how many stream fishermen tie on small poppers and chuggers, because "smallmouths have small mouths." What nonsense.

Any smallmouth measuring 15 or more inches will flaunt a sizeable maw, and such a predator knows how to use it. My topwater tackle box for river smallmouths contains many of the same size lures and flies that my corresponding lake tackle box does.

Second, although a frog pattern embossed my Rapala Skitter Prop that day, it is the size, shape, and action of the bait or fly that matters—not its

Some fly and spin fishermen do like it hot.

color. I choose color patterns for lures and flies because they are pleasing to me, and because they are attractive, I use them more often. The smallmouths that feverishly attacked the Skitter Prop that day would have done so if it had had a saber tooth tiger, an elephant, or a crow embossed on its sides.

Third, rotate among your topwater baits and flies. In my canoe, I always have at least two spinning rods, sometimes three, adorned with topwaters, as well as a long rod equipped with a surface pattern. Sometimes, the smallmouths will prefer prop baits like the Skitter Prop, Tiny Torpedo, and Crippled Killer. Other days, they will favor stick baits such as Chug Bugs and Zara Spooks. On others, the whirling motion of a buzzbait will raise their hackles. And sometimes, the bass will only want the subtle action of a deer hair bug or a damselfly imitation.

For instance, during the aforementioned day when the smallies were ravaging the Skitter Prop in the early afternoon, by mid-afternoon, only the buzzer could bring topwater strikes. Let the bass tell you which type of topwater or fly they prefer at any given hour of the post-noon period.

Areas to Target

If you want to catch hordes of 8- to 10-inch smallmouths, tie on a pint-sized inline spinner, a 1½-inch white grub, or a size 10 cricket and paddle toward the nearest 2-foot-deep riffle. You should be able to boat about two dozen fish within a few hours. If you want to tangle with some bronzeback behemoths, then head for some very specific places.

Perhaps the favorite haunt of midday summertime river bass is a deep-water ledge lying in at least five feet of liquid. If that ledge lies within or adjacent to the main channel and is just downstream from a rapid, then the potential for this locale is even greater. I like to position my canoe downstream and sideways in the current (so as to slow its drift) and cast lures and flies just beyond either where a ledge breaks the surface or creates a dark shadow beneath. The sweet spot is the "green water" immediately below the rock structure.

Another marvelous locale is an outside bend that features a heavily wooded bank. If that is the case, then you can expect downed trees and exposed roots to provide excellent shoreline cover. Add scattered boulders along the shore and at least basketball-sized rocks in the immediate vicinity, and the potential is obvious. Target the little patches of shade that form because of the angle of the noonday sun.

The third hot spot is an eddy adjacent to swift water. Dave Arnold calls these "eddy pockets," and they are superlative places to find active midday mossybacks. The reversing currents of eddy pockets traps minnows, hellgrammites, crayfish, and assorted other aquatic creatures.

If the Topwater Bite Wanes

Even the most belligerent summertime stream bass will sometimes refuse to fin toward the surface. When that happens, I primarily turn to soft plastic baits, Clouser Minnows, or Woolly Buggers. For instance, one year while on a junket down Virginia's South Fork of the Shenandoah, I enjoyed solid early afternoon activity while employing topwaters. But when the topwater bite waned, I opted for a deep-water pattern.

On that outing, I turned to 4-inch tubes and began probing a series of deep-water ledges. Smallies up to 18 inches fell for the tubes, and I caught a number more in the 12- to 16-inch range. Later in the day, I had to make another bait change to extend the bite—this time to 6-inch plastic worms.

Besides tubes and worms, other excellent soft plastic baits are 4-inch craw worms, 5-inch grubs, and 6-inch lizards. I rig all these baits Texas style with 2/0 Daiichi Bleeding Bait hooks in the offset configuration. A ¼-ounce sliding sinker completes the rig. Regarding rods and reels, I favor

6½-foot medium heavy action baitcasters and spinning rods, spooled with 10- or 12-pound test. And if the soft plastic bait bite slows, throw the bass another change of pace by tying on medium depth running crankbaits that are at least ¼-ounce. Again, ultralight lures and tackle have no place in your game plan if you are after big river bass in the afternoon.

Fly fishermen similarly have a number of choices when the topwater bite slows. For instance, North Carolina's Kevin Howell, who operates Davidson River Outfitters (www.davidsonflyfishing.com), maintains that streamers are excellent choices when the bass are still in the chasing mood but not inclined to rise to the surface. Among his favorites are Walker's Wiggler in olive and white, Clouser Minnow in olive and white, Black Bunny Leech, olive Woolly Bugger, and white lead eye Woolly Bugger. If you have a hankering to cast some fetching baits and flies to some very ample river smallmouths, then you may well find why some of us moving water anglers like the hot action of the hottest time of a summer day.

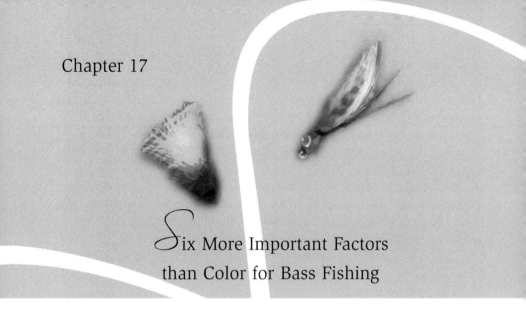

Chapter 17

Six More Important Factors than Color for Bass Fishing

Recently before I was to give a bass fishing seminar, the host of the affair asked what my favorite lure/fly color was for fooling bass. In a fit of honesty—or perhaps annoyance from having that same question posed so often—I responded that I buy colors that please me and that I seriously doubt if color matters to largemouth, smallmouth, or spotted bass the vast majority of the time. And that's true, I added, regardless of whether these black bass fin lakes, rivers, ponds, or streams—or whether one goes after bass with a baitcaster, fly rod, spinning rod, or cane pole.

"Don't tell them that," gasped the host. "It will get everybody all upset."

That exchange made me think about what really is relevant concerning whether or not we catch bass. Here are what I consider to be the seven major factors—with color being last on the list.

1: Location

We have all heard the real estate cliché that the three most important factors about whether a property will sell are "location, location, location." Actually, the same adage holds true for bass fishing. For example, throughout most of the year, quality bass will restrict themselves to relatively few places on a lake, reservoir, or river. Humps, main channel drop-offs, deep-water ledges, points of various kinds, and rock, vegetation, and wood cover in deep water (relative to the overall depth of the body of water) are gold standards just about anywhere in the country.

Let's face facts. Except for the spawn, most of the time, on most of America's waters, most of the quality bass will be holding in one of those places. Find those spots on your home fishing hole, and you're in business.

2: Presentation

We have all experienced times when the person at the other end of the boat was catching bass and we were not, even though we had been tossing the same lures and flies to the same places. Chances are quite high that our buddy did not have a magic colored bait or some secret fly, as we often want to believe, but that he was working his artificial in such a way as to make the fish strike.

Presentation matters. Stop-and-start a crankbait, snap pop a popper, cut capers with a chugger, flutter a spinnerbait, lift-pause a worm—in short, do something to make your bait or fly more appealing (and give it a different look) to the fish. Experiment with rigs and especially the speed and angle of a retrieve. Mindlessly chunking and winding rarely works.

3: Water Temperature

Understanding how bass react to changes in water temperature is the factor I rate the third most critical. For instance, in the spring marvelous fishing will often ensue if the water temperature increases a few degrees. Come early fall, a few degrees drop can make the bass more active. Look for those places that are either warmer or colder, depending on the season, than the vast majority of a lake or river; chances are that you will have found active bass.

4: Season

Bass fishing is one of the most logical pastimes I know. Bass behave in certain predictable ways at certain times of the year and that is a fact. On both lakes and rivers, for example, wintertime bass will hold tight to the main channel or at the ends of long points that have precipitous drops. Come summer, the fish often move shallow early in the day but typically retreat to deeper water as the sun rises higher on the horizon.

The above information certainly isn't new, but I often find it surprising that many anglers want the fish to conform to their preconceived notions of where the bass should be. Learn the basic seasonal patterns of bass, and you will catch more fish than 90 percent of the anglers on your home water do.

5: Frontal Conditions

Many anglers could make a pretty fair argument that frontal conditions should rank higher than fifth on our factor countdown, and I wouldn't disagree. Give us a warm front, a stable barometer, and rising water temperature in the spring, and the odds are good that we will catch some hefty fish. Put most anglers, this writer included, on a body of water where a cold front is taking place, the sky is blue, and the air and water temperatures are decreasing, and chances are equally high that fishing success rates will be low.

Here are some more facts to face. Most of us can catch bass during a warm front; multiple patterns will produce fish, and even anglers with modest skills should be able to score. If a classic, cold front clobbers an area, even professional anglers and guides will likely struggle. If the fish are truly inactive, they simply will not be feeding and the best any of us can hope for is the occasional reaction strike. Inactive fish—by definition—are not feeders.

What outdoor writers really should state when they are writing about how to catch inactive bass is "how to catch bass in a neutral feeding mode." America's best anglers are those individuals who can entice fish that are not turned on, but that aren't turned off either.

6: Lure and Fly Choice

Here are some simple truths about fishing lures and flies—there is no such thing as magic ones. There is no artificial that we can buy that will automatically turn us into better anglers. Lures and flies are merely tools for catching bass, and certain tools work better under certain situations, seasons, and conditions than others do.

Does the color of a fly really matter? Most of the time, no.

If the first five factors mentioned above are in our favor, do you really think that whether, for example, we toss a worm, craw worm, lizard, and tube, or surface flies, streamers, or nymphs to a downed tree really matters? All we really have to learn about lures and flies is which ones generally work best under certain situations.

7: Color

In all my years of fishing, I can recall only one outing where color might have made a difference. Don't waste time agonizing about "matching the hatch" when fishing for bass; after all, they aren't trout. Buy baits and flies in the colors that you have confidence in. For example, my favorite color is orange/brown. Many of the fish I catch are caught on lures or flies in this color—not because of the hue itself, but because I use baits and flies in that shade more often. If you believe that a crankbait in a rhinoceros pattern works best or a streamer colored like a zebra will produce for you, then you will be successful with that pattern.

I repeat—fishing is a logical pastime. Bass have very small brains, and they act in predicable and logical ways. What we won't always definitively know on any given day is how they will act at the time we are fishing for them. And figuring out a pattern is one of the great joys of this pastime.

Regarding color, anglers often waste time agonizing over color— whether they should paint a lure or own a lure in several shades, or what the "hot" color is on a certain lake. On any given excursion, make sure you have factored in the first six factors before you begin to agonize about color.

Summing Up: The Most Essential Item in a Tackle Box

A $2 water temperature thermometer is the most essential item I have in my arsenal. Yes, I know that some very expensive versions can be purchased to affix to a boat, but they all perform the same function. Check a water temperature gauge throughout the day and at different locations. Chances are that a pattern will emerge, and you can use that information to be more successful—all because of an inexpensive gizmo.

For example, on a trip to a local body of water, a buddy and I once encountered difficult fishing during the pre-spawn period. We caught bass sporadically around stumps during the day, but it was not until we began taking water temperature readings that we understood how we could do much better. Only those stumps that were on the lee sides and resting in water at least two degrees warmer than the surrounding environs produced fish.

Once we implemented our stumps-plus-two-degrees pattern, we caught fish consistently. That outing was a prime example of three of the more important factors (location, presentation, and water temperature) coming into play.

Chapter 18

*C*huggers:
Great Lures and Flies for Warm Season Bass

In the closet of my work room, some 25 tackle boxes of various sizes lie on the floor and on top of each other. Seven of those boxes accommodate just topwater lures and flies, and one of those containers only houses 11 surface offerings But if my home were on fire and I could only save one tackle box, it would be that latter one. Within that box are my very favorite topwater artificials—the ones that have produced for years (and in some cases decades) and that I often tie on when I really, really need a nice bass.

And among those 11 lures, one especially stands out; it is a Rebel Pop-R, which I got in 1991. This chugger sports the profile of a bait ravaged by numerous bass, as all of the paint has been smashed off its head and about a fourth of the upper body. The feathers on the rear treble began to disappear in the mid-1990s and were totally gone by the end of the century. All across the rest of the lure are pockmarks from where various bass have crushed it.

Obviously, I am a fan of hard plastic chugger-style baits, both of the lure and fly variety. I asked Chris Gulstad, public relations manager for PRADCO, to define just what constitutes a chugger.

"Basically, chuggers have open concave lip surfaces that produce popping, gurgling sounds when they are retrieved across the surface," he said. "I think a major reason they are so productive is the sounds that they produce. Chuggers 'call' to bass and thus help the fish locate them on several different sensory levels. First, the bass can 'feel' the chugger moving across the surface with their lateral lines.

"Second, they can hear the popping, gurgling sounds as it skitters across the surface. And, finally, chuggers offer very strong visual clues.

For example, if you have ever seen bass chasing minnows, baitfish, or shad across the surface, you know how stimulating it is for bass to see creatures fleeing from them. That fleeing motion stimulates the feeding response even in turned-off bass. They are conditioned to hit things that move like chuggers."

Gulstad explained that several types of chuggers exist. The first consists of shallow divers: creations which when pulled take a quick plunge under water and then pop to the surface, often spitting, gurgling, or otherwise moving water as they do so. Besides the Rebel Pop-R, other artificials in this category include the Heddon Lucky 13, the Rapala Skitter Pop, the Excalibur Pop-N-Image, and the Mann's Two-Fer.

In the second category, continues Gulstad, is the type of chugger that when retrieved makes a relatively deep dive and then pops up— meanwhile displacing a great deal of water. A good example of this type lure is the Arbogast Hula Popper—that traditional favorite of generations of rural farm boys as they prowl ponds during the summer months. The final category is made up of what I call hybrid chuggers. These topwaters feature the same concave lips but they typically have long, slim bodies, as well. A good example of this category is the Storm Chug Bug, which can be worked like the standard chugger but can also be retrieved in the classic walk-the-dog motion.

Fly rod chuggers are much simpler in design but just as effective. They are typically an inch long or less, not including hackle, and sport a concave lip. Harry Murray's Gray and Chartreuse Chuggars (sic) are excellent examples of this, and noted smallmouth long rod expert Tim Holschlag also makes a dandy chugger, to name a few.

Whichever category of chugger you prefer, one thing is certain, they command a great deal of loyalty from their owners. I told Gulstad that many times I had climbed out of my boat or into a tree to retrieve my favorite models. He was not surprised to hear of my exploits.

"People can become very fond of certain, individual lures and flies, especially topwater ones like chuggers," said Gulstad. "Over time, fishermen develop great confidence in chuggers after seeing the bass strike them in a very visual manner as they typically do on the surface."

The Standard Plop and Pause

If an angler could perfect just one way to bring in a chugger, then it would have to be the standard plop-and-pause gambit. When a red hot summer topwater bite (or, for that matter, even a lukewarm one) is going on, this retrieve will work a high percentage of the time.

For the plop and pause, I like to cast about five yards past my target, and then launch into a medium-paced retrieve. I never stop the retrieve for more than a few seconds and never slow or accelerate the pace when a bass takes a swipe at the chugger and misses. Another appealing fact about this type of retrieve is that a bass is just as likely to hit a chugger as soon as it touches down, when it approaches cover, when it leaves cover, or even when the chugger nears a boat. Just keep this creation, dare I say, "chugging along" at a moderate pace and expect a strike at any time.

The Rapid Fire Spit

The rapid fire spit retrieve is an aggressive maneuver that seems to work best when the bass are in a neutral mode. That is, the bass are present, they are holding along predictable forms of cover, but, for whatever reason, the fish just aren't hitting our offerings at the time. This tactic, though, will shake them out of their summertime doldrums. To begin this retrieve, I point my rod tip down close to the water, reel in the slack, and then begin to quickly strip in line (or reel in line with a spinning rod) while simultaneously making short, quick, hard jerking motions while continuing to pick up line.

This fine smallmouth fell for a chugger—a great option for river smallmouth fans.

As the chugger careens across the surface, it gives off very noticeable sprays of water, that is, it spits. Bass will awaken from their neutral states and smash a spitting chugger. Once again, if a bass misses a chugger retrieved in this manner, don't change what you are doing. Oftentimes a fish will come back and maul the offering much more savagely than it did the first time when it missed. Several times, I have experienced a bass smashing a chugger three or four times before a hookup resulted.

The Near-Death Retrieve

Obviously, the near-death retrieve is the easiest to implement. This tactic works best when the bass are holding tight to specific forms of cover and when the water either has a slight chop to it or is slightly to moderately stained. The bass are sort of in a feeding mood, but they also have to be coaxed into rising from their lairs.

When all these conditions are in play, cast your chugger directly to the cover form and let it sit for 20, 30, or more seconds. Then make your bait or fly emit a gentle bloop and let it rest for another long interval. One caveat—I rarely have had bass come back a second time on the near-death retrieve. Chances are that you'll get one chance—and one chance only— to set the hook. Be ready.

The Walk-the-Dog Scenario

You can walk the dog with almost any chugger, but the long slim models perform this gambit much better than the short, squat versions do. This type of retrieve is very much a rhythmic one. Sometimes on any given day, anglers may even have to make four or five casts before they find their groove. But once they figure out the right rhythm and the chugger moves back and forth, side to side in a very predictable manner, the results can be quite impressive.

The walk-the-dog scenario has the ability to fetch bass from long distances, particularly when the water is clear and even when the fish have been under a great deal of pressure. Interestingly, bass will often "porpoise" along the surface for several yards before they finally crush a chugger returned in this manner. Also, sometimes this retrieve will attract several bass at once.

Topwater Targets

One of the remarkable things about chuggers is that they can be fished around both structure and cover and even across open water. For example, let's say that the time is mid-August and you have determined that the bass are holding on the first break line out from the bank, along drop-offs down a point, or on main channel drop-offs—all classic and common forms of structure.

For the break line scenario, position the bow of your boat perpendicular to the bank and bring your chugger across the break. For both of the drop-off situations, place your boat parallel to the structure and retrieve the chugger down the drop-offs.

Chuggers are equally adept at extracting summer bass from cover, which may come in the form of various kinds of vegetation, downed trees lying perpendicular or parallel to the shoreline, underwater brush piles, flotsam that has accumulated in eddies, docks, and various other forms of human-made cover. For both these structure and cover situations, experiment with the types of retrieves detailed above until you find the one that the fish favor on that particular outing.

Chuggers even produce bass in open water situations. All of the retrieves listed above can come into play except the near-death one, as cruising open water bass rarely seem to find appeal in a motionless object. Perhaps the best retrieve for these open water fish is the rapid one. It is also quite good when you are not sure where the bass are but you do know that they are present somewhere over a considerable expanse.

Time of Day

I do not believe in the conventional wisdom that proclaims summertime mornings and evenings as the only time periods when topwaters, specifically chuggers, can produce their magic. I also don't accept the premise that only certain types of retrieves will work at certain times of the day.

For example, several summers ago, a buddy and I arrived at my home body of water about 45 minutes before sunrise and discovered upon launching that a tremendous topwater bite was in play. My buddy and I threw poppers, chuggers, slim minnow imitations, and buzzbaits in a variety of places at a variety of speeds, and every gambit we tried succeeded.

Later that morning, we tossed chuggers around both rock and wood cover and continued to catch bass. When the midday sun forced the bass either deep along the main channel or tight to the bank in shade pockets, my friend and I continued to catch bass with chuggers and other surface creations. And late in the evening and right before we ended our outing, the two of us employed chuggers and buzzbaits to fan cast points and also flats adjacent to the main channel.

My point is that chuggers are not just low light lures. Summertime bass have not read the book of conventional wisdom, and they hit our offerings because they are actually hungry or because they just feel like it. Look for a chugger bite throughout a summertime day. Indeed, chuggers can continue to be effective well past Labor Day most years.

And if you are one of those anglers whose home river has an exceptional amount of pleasure boat and fishing traffic on weekends and prefer to visit it after work during the weekdays or after dark on weekends, the chugger is a marvelous option late in the evening and after dark. For instance, a good friend of mine and I went to our home lake several years ago after work on a Friday. About 20 minutes before sunset, the chugger bite began as my buddy located fish that were cruising a grass bed. But the bite continued well after dark when the fish moved tight to the shoreline and held around chunk rock and downed trees. The blooping sounds of chuggers are real fish callers before and after sunset.

Hooks for Lures

If there is one downside about the chuggers made by many companies it is that their hooks are just generic trebles that often lack sharpness and durability. (Conversely, the fly rod chuggers I've used have all had quality hooks.) Many hooks are of such poor quality that no matter how diligent we are about touching them up with a sharpener, we still won't achieve the desired result of more hookups.

That's why I almost always replace the factory hooks on most of my chuggers. Several hook companies manufacture extremely sharp, long lasting trebles, and they often can result in our hooking and, just as importantly, landing many more bass than before.

Some anglers like to replace the factory trebles with hooks one size larger. Sometimes this approach works, but sometimes it also destroys the delicate balance between hook and lure. Regardless of whether you replace the factory hooks with trebles a size larger or the same size, try out your new creations in a swimming pool or pond before heading for a lake. If the chuggers aren't spitting and blooping like they were previously, have them undergo another operation.

Rods and Reels

Some anglers prefer baitcasters for chuggers while others opt for spinning rods. Some fishermen like 7-foot rods while others select ones that run 6½ feet. All of these schools of thought have their virtues, but I do believe that rods should have two qualities above all.

First, for best results, chugger rods should be medium action. When a bass savages a chugger from underneath or from behind, an angler needs a rod with some give in it so that the bait is not as easily pulled from a bass' mouth—as is too often the case with medium heavy or heavy action rods.

Second, I believe that using the same rod, regardless of type, for all your chuggers will result in catching more bass. For example, my favorite chugger rod is one I have owned for nearly 20 years and a model that its company stopped making more than 15 years ago. The rod is a medium action spinning one, and every year I hope to coax one more season out of it before it finally breaks. This rod excels at allowing me to effectively use all the various kinds of retrieves.

Long rodders need only the popular 8½-foot rod (medium stiff, medium fast action) with a 7 or 8 weight bass bug taper fly line. Nine-foot tapered monofilament leaders with a tippet strength of 10-pound test are sufficient.

Summing Up

During most of the 1980s, bass anglers infrequently used chuggers, and one of the most legendary poppers of all time—the Rebel Pop-R—was so out of favor that it was not even manufactured for a time. But, lo and behold, the few chuggers that were still around began to produce some important tournament victories and by the early 1990s, these lures were experiencing a rebirth.

Today, some 15 years later, the chugger remains a must-have bait in most anglers' tackle boxes and one that is amazingly adept at catching fish under a variety of situations. And if you are a fan of chuggers as I am, after you rescue your family from a burning home, you'll take the time to go back for your box of productive chuggers.

Part Four:

Fall Smallmouth Fishing

Chapter 19

$\mathcal{F}$ive Top Lures and Flies for Fall Smallies

For many smallmouth anglers, fall is one of their most (and least) favorite times of the year. The former circumstance holds true when the water is green tinted to stained, when the frontal conditions are stationary or a warm front is on the way, and when the water temperature is steady or at least not fluctuating wildly.

But the latter circumstance is true too much of the time and actually, unfortunately, is probably the normal state of affairs. That is because the fall period, especially October, is the most likely time of year for the water to be extremely clear and usually low. Then smallmouth bass, particularly the larger specimens, can become maddeningly difficult to entice. With that latter circumstance in mind, here are five choice lures and their fly counterparts for autumn brown bass.

Plastic Worms and Nymphs: Split Shot Them

Throughout the 1960s and most of the 1970s, the 6-inch soft plastic curly tail worm, rigged on a sliding bullet sinker, was the gold standard for largemouth anglers across the country. Then and now, smallmouth anglers have never been as big of fans of the bogus crawler as their largemouth brethren, but perhaps they should be. For the clear water conditions of fall are excellent times to employ a plastic worm.

However, I would suggest not rigging it Texas style for the unique conditions we smallmouth anglers contend with nor would I opt for the 6-inch size or a bullet sinker. My choice would be a 4-inch curly or straight tail worm with a split shot placed some 12 to 18 inches above it.

A bullet sinker simply causes too much water disturbance in low, clear water, especially on impact. Baits rigged Texas style or weedless have their place, even for smallmouth anglers, of course, but again—because of the tough conditions and the likelihood of a light bite—a better option would be to skin hook a worm or even have the hook tip slightly exposed.

I would also recommend the four-inch curly or straight tail worm. What the smaller worm does offer is less commotion when it enters the water column. And it provides a less threatening profile when a wary, clear-water smallie is eyeing this artificial lying or slowly inching or drifting across the bottom. Smallish worms are "fool 'em" baits, and the tinier the worms are, the more enticing they are to hesitant fish.

The split shot rig is just a downsized, less obtrusive form of the Carolina rig and is an ideal choice for highly transparent water. Think of those long ago days when you placed a real nightcrawler under a split shot and caught plenty of fish with the getup. A split shot worm is not all that different. Split shot worms are great baits to fish across rocky bottoms and during the midday period when the bite slows.

Fly fishermen should consider placing a split shot above a nymph or having the pattern tied with a bead head. Kevin Howell, who operates Davidson River Outfitters, told me that he uses a number of different nymphs for stream smallies. Among his favorites are Howell's Big Nasty, Howell's Ole Hellgy, Clouser Crayfish, Howell's Stoneymite, and Yuk Bug.

What's more, these patterns are not just for fall angling. They can entice stream smallmouths throughout the year, even during the dead of winter. Nymphs certainly aren't glamorous patterns, but they can produce quality smallmouths. For example, on one journey, a friend and I both started out using poppers. I was determined that I could convince smallies to rise to the surface.

But about half way through our outing, my buddy forsook the surface option and switched to a weighted nymph in a crayfish pattern. The friend ended up salvaging the day by catching and releasing two keeper-sized smallies. My best fish was a scrawny nine-incher.

Crayfish Imitations

For the past decade at least, the tube has quite probably been the most popular soft plastic bait among the smallmouth crowd. Nothing, I would wager, even comes close—certainly not worms, craw worms, or lizards—with the possible exception of a soft plastic jerkbait. The 4-inch tube, rigged Texas style, is often the choice of anglers who pursue trophy smallies.

Fall is one of the best times to experience America's smallmouth rivers, and knowing which flies and lures to use can make that experience even better.

Again, though, because of the conditions, I would not opt for a weedless tube at this time of year. A better choice would be a 4-inch tube rigged on a ¼-, ⅛-, or ¹⁄₁₆-ounce jighead with the point skin hooked so it is barely exposed and tight against the lure. While I would recommend leaving the split shot worm in one place for long periods of time, I would fairly aggressively hop a tube on a jighead across the bottom.

And that's where the jighead comes into play. Jigheads enable us to assertively bring the bait through the water column, much like a crayfish fleeing for its life. Indeed, a jighead-rigged tube looks much like a terrified crawdad desperate to return beneath a rock. The bigger size of this lure, just like in the spring and summer, is also a real enticement for bigger brownies.

Similarly, a crayfish pattern, such as a Clouser Crayfish and Tim's HiTail Craw, is an outstanding autumn choice. Here's a little tip. Don't go overboard with realism; smallmouths become wary when they encounter crayfish with large pincers. A crayfish deploys those claws as weapons, and a smallie instinctively knows that. If you tie your own flies, go easy on the hackle needed for the claws. If you buy your patterns, consider trimming back the bogus claws.

Work a tube on a jighead or a crayfish pattern parallel to weed beds, specifically if they are still green. Also toss this duo to the outside edges of brush piles, beaver lodges, and downed trees.

Grubs on a Jighead, Streamers on a Sink Tip

When many of us, including this writer, first began angling for smallmouths, the standard 3-inch grub was the first soft plastic bait that we used. Once we became more "sophisticated," this artificial quickly fell out of our favor. Well, just as it was in our earlier days, a grub remains a fish-catching machine of a bait and is another effective choice for clear water.

Grubs are primarily swim baits—lures that can be brought back with the current (and just about all lakes and rivers in our region have at least some degree of current or wind action). In the spring and summer, grubs mainly draw aggressive fish, but now I like them for their ability to catch smallies of all sizes and both aggressive and neutral ones.

If a clear-water smallmouth, especially at dawn or dusk, spots a grub quickly swimming by in the water column, the fish will very possibly attack it. If a neutral bass glimpses this soft plastic concoction dashing by it in the middle of the day, chances are that it will dash out to nip it—and that's where the exposed hook of a jighead will come into play. Retrieving a grub past any form of cover works, but grubs really excel at being fan cast across a wide area. Sooner or later this lure will pass by a willing mossyback.

Similarly, streamers were the first subsurface fly many long rodders tied on when they made the first decision to probe beneath the surface. I remember buying my first streamer, a Silver Outcast, and affixing it to my regular fly line. I was amazed at how much the fly, when stripped just beneath the surface, moved like the darting dace and minnows common in the creek.

Today, serious long rodders often work streamers, such as the Clouser Minnow and Shenk's White Streamer, on sink tip lines. Compared to casting a topwater fly, using a sink tip line is hard work and not much fun—until a hookup occurs.

Poppers: Both the Lure and Fly Varieties

After a number of years of fishing on a very clear body of water, a buddy badly-out fished me by using a popper as his go-to choice throughout the day. I kept proclaiming that it was too late in the fall for a strong topwater bite to be occurring, and my friend kept proving me wrong. I was too proud to tie on a popper that day, but ever since I have used these lures and flies with success during the autumn period.

If a smallie addict will stop to consider why poppers perform well, he will be more likely to utilize them. What this surface creation basically communicates is that it is a medium size, dying creature struggling about on the surface. It is no wonder then that a smallmouth will charge upwards five, ten, or more feet from the bottom to smash one.

Some anglers opt to jiggle a motionless popper, barely dimpling the water surface while doing so. Others like to leave one motionless for long periods, then violently cause it to career across the surface. Others pop the popper across the top at regular intervals. Poppers work equally well over deep, rocky pools and along the shoreline or weed beds. Don't let the water temperature deter you from fishing one. As is usually the case, the fish will tell you which tactic is best on a given day.

Minnow Imitations: Suspend Them

Weighted sculpins and hard plastic minnow jerkbaits have long been standard wintertime patterns and lures among the smallmouth brigade, but we should recognize that this duo works extremely well during the autumn, too. A major reason is that a subsurface minnow imitation enables an angler to work it in two distinctive ways.

For example, a sculpin/jerkbait can be retrieved rapidly through the water column and cause a fish to instinctively lash out and hit it. Or a bogus baitfish can brought back via the stop-and-go method, which often results in a smallmouth sipping it in while the offering is paused or begins to slowly rise to the surface. In this manner, a hard plastic jerkbait is not all that different from a soft plastic stickbait—except the former slowly rises to the surface while the latter slowly sinks. The key word, though, is slow, and that is why a lethargic smallie will often be tempted into tasting a hard plastic jerkbait or a sculpin pattern.

Prime places to work sculpins/jerkbaits include main channel drop-offs, across humps and points, and through rocky pools.

Ideally, we would be able to fish in green or slightly stained water the entire fall. Such is not the case most years and likely will not be so this year either. That is why these five fly and lure choices should be considered essentials in a fall smallmouth angler's tackle box.

Chapter 20

*B*ass Fishing's All-Purpose Bait: The Grub

One of the mysteries of American bass fishing is why a grub is called a *grub*. After all, this soft plastic bait looks nothing like its namesake in either size or color—that little grayish-white creature that lives underground and is the larval form of various species of insects. Perhaps another mystery is why grubs are such effective baits for bass throughout the year—even during the winter months.

Overview of the Grub

I asked Al Kalin, who operates the Kalin Company, a manufacturer of soft plastic baits, why grubs catch fish.

"All I know is that they work in cold water, and they work in warm," Kalin told me. "The reason why they catch bass might be the way a grub wiggles when it is retrieved. And that wiggle is key. If the soft plastic is such that it becomes hard and brittle, instead of soft and supple, in cold water, then the bait definitely won't attract fish."

Kalin says that lure popularity typically comes and goes, and that right now the grub is not a popular artificial, which, ironically, makes it a more effective lure for bass since they don't see it as often—especially during the winter months. Kalin believes that Mann's Stingray Grub, a flat tail bait, may have been one of the first popular lures in this category, along with the curl tail version that Mister Twister sold. In any event, the grub apparently was an offshoot of the craze for worm fishing that American bass fishing experienced in the 1950s and 1960s. Really, continues Kalin, a grub is nothing more than a small worm with a tail.

Grubs are among the most versatile of lures for the river smallmouth fisherman.

Kalin says that grubs reached their peak popularity in the 1980s when companies such as Yamamoto and his own, among others, experienced solid sales. Ever since then, grub sales have declined as newer, sexier baits, such as the soft plastic jerkbaits in the early 1990s and big tubes and Senko-style lures currently, have dominated the attentions of bass fishermen.

Kalin noted "If 95 percent of bass fishermen use a particular style of bait, 95 percent of the fish will be caught on that bait. That doesn't mean that grubs still won't catch fish. No matter where you fish in this country, no matter the season, grubs still work."

Styles: The 3-inch Grub on a Jighead

By far, my favorite way to fish a grub is to attach a 3-inch version to either a ¼ or ⅛-ounce jighead. An anecdote from my initial fishing trip of the New Year one winter shows why. Bluebird skies, a cold front, and close-mouthed bass were the story; I spent a long, frustrating morning with only two keeper-sized fish landed, and those two barely met the minimum size limit.

Not knowing what the pattern was and with only 90 minutes of fishing time left, I decided to attach a 3-inch grub to a ¼-ounce jighead and fan cast the area I was fishing. During that time period, I tangled with a pair of two-pound bass. Though these two fish were certainly not huge, they saved my outing and were quality fish given the conditions and the season.

Those wintertime bass were holding in a deep, rocky pool adjacent to the main channel. A good tactic for this situation is to allow the grub/jighead to sink to the bottom and then slowly retrieve the bait just fast enough to keep it above the rocks. This same rig will also work when bass are more active and move into the current of the main channel.

The 5-inch Grub Rigged Texas Style

Bass fishermen rig just about every soft plastic concoction Texas style, but we infrequently make a grub weedless. Nevertheless, a 5-inch grub rigged weedless and with a sliding bullet sinker is a superlative wintertime lure.

For example, during the cold water period, bass often move into very heavy cover to await better foraging conditions. Examples of this type of habitat include brush piles, logjams, and beaver huts. A 3-inch grub on a jighead is simply not going to pass through this type of cover, but a Texas-rigged 5-inch grub can nestle down into the thick stuff and be inched through it. The latter can also be left motionless for long periods of time, moved forward a short distance, and then once again be left to slumber. Sooner or later, a lethargic bass may well decide that a 5-inch grub offers the size and bulk to make the fish move from its winter lair. Of all the baits mentioned in this story, I would rate the 5-inch grub as the one most likely to attract larger winter bass.

Another place to use this lure is on drop-offs out from weedbeds. Of course, the weedbeds themselves will likely not be green or growing. But if the shelves where the vegetation flourishes during the warm water period are either adjacent or relatively near deeper water, the bass may be holding on the first major drop out from them.

Curl Tail Grubs on a Carolina Rig

Two of the most important river smallmouth wintering grounds are deep, rocky pools and main channel drop-offs. Both these locales offer deep water with relatively stable conditions, which is something benumbed bass crave. And certainly one of the best ways to prospect for bass in these two situations is with 3-inch, 4-inch, or 5-inch curl tail grubs on Carolina rigs.

During the warm water period, many bass fishermen like to work rocky pools and main channel drop-offs at a fairly fast clip. In the winter months, though, I would suggest going at the slowest pace you can stand. I would also recommend that whatever length grub you decide to use, that you not rig it weedless. Deep water, wintertime bites are extremely light and accomplishing a good hookup under the prevailing conditions is very difficult.

I also believe that it is imperative that the egg sinker part of the Carolina rig always maintain contact with the bottom. During the warm water period, we can get away with the sinker occasionally rising off the bottom. Wintertime bass are not as forgiving and far less likely to chase a bait that is much over their heads.

Flat-Tailed Grubs as Finesse Baits

The closer the water temperature is to freezing, the greater the likelihood that the bass will be inactive or at best in a neutral feeding mode. This is especially true if the water temperature has been dropping instead of rising. For this condition, a 3-inch flat tail grub is an excellent option.

Sometimes called straight-tailed grubs, this lure is nothing more than a short worm with a paddle tail. Often flat tails are attached to a slider head or some other jighead that is designed to be dragged along the bottom. I like to rig flat-tailed grubs weedless because of the great danger of snags, but, in any event, expect to lose plenty of baits. This is another wintertime lure that cannot be retrieved too slowly.

Also expect this grub rig to be one of the few workable options for very lethargic wintertime bass. Anticipate the fish being in heavy shoreline cover such as logjams and deep-water woody debris of all kinds.

Drop Shotting Grubs

Drop shotting has become one of the hottest ways to rig soft plastic baits, and it is not surprising that this getup has a cold water application. I prefer a 3-inch curl tail grub for this rig, although larger baits will certainly perform well.

As is true with the Carolina rig, you may have to use larger sinkers in the wintertime on your home stream in order to maintain tight contact with the bottom. Also, instead of slowly retrieving a grub that is drop shot, consider leaving the bait in place and slowly raising and lowering it a few inches. Good places to try this gambit are bars, points, and ledges, all, of course, in deep water relative to your local stream.

Color and Rod and Reel Options

For wintertime grub fishing, I believe that color is especially irrelevant while rod and reel choice is important. A medium or medium-heavy spinning rod is a logical choice when fan casting a 3-inch grub on a jighead, given this bait's light weight. For 5-inch grubs rigged Texas style, a medium heavy baitcaster receives the nod. For all other rigs, medium heavy spinning or baitcasters work equally well.

In a decade, maybe two, the grub will come back into fashion and once again receive national acclaim. Right now, for wintertime fishing, the grub is certainly one of the best options that we bass anglers can turn to with confidence.

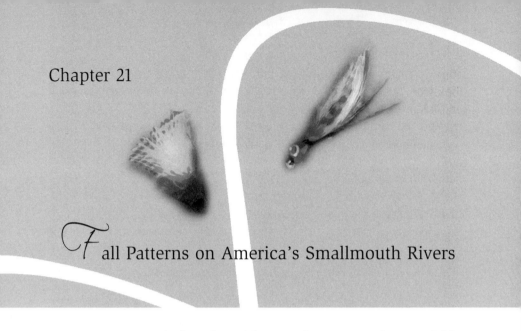

Chapter 21

$\mathcal{F}$all Patterns on America's Smallmouth Rivers

As our country's best bass lakes receive more and more fishing pressure, more and more anglers are turning to America's smallmouth rivers for their angling pleasure. And autumn is certainly a wonderful time to experience the distinct pleasure of moving-water bassing.

But just as lake largemouths can be maddeningly difficult to catch during this transitional and ever-changing season, so can stream smallmouths. Here, then, are five major patterns you can implement, should you journey to a bronzeback bastion this fall.

Ultra Clear Water/Topwater Pattern

The ultra clear water/topwater pattern is most likely to occur—and be strongest—during the early stages of autumn. After a long, hot, dry summer, many rivers are at their lowest water levels of the year now.

A veteran angler taught me how to exploit this pattern a number of years ago. We journeyed to a dandy mossyback stream where I went without a nice smallie the entire morning. I relied on the same offerings that had produced so well just a few weeks earlier during the tail end of summer.

Meanwhile, my boat mate deftly analyzed the situation. He saw the bass either flee or get spooked by my crankbaits, spinnerbaits, and soft plastics. So he resorted to tossing Heddon Tiny Torpedoes well back under the leafy canopies of trees that shrouded the shoreline.

Furthermore, my friend (given the low, clear liquid) deigned not to allow these prop baits to rest for even a second. After the lures touched down, they were quickly churned across the surface. His goal was to not let the bass too closely inspect these lures. Indeed, the times he let a

Torpedo linger under an overhanging tree limb, the lure received a quick look from a smallmouth, which then turned immediately away. I had to endure my buddy catching four nice smallmouths before I summoned enough common sense to copy his pattern.

The clear water/topwater pattern often does not last past mid-fall and/or until the water temperature sinks permanently below 58 to 60 degrees. Generally, the smallies will stop hitting rapidly moving artificials such as buzzbaits and streamers first, but will continue to engulf prop baits, poppers, chuggers, and stick baits for a while longer. I have experienced almost no success with topwaters, either with a fly rod or spinning rod, in late fall.

Also, my friend's penchant for seeking out shade is very relevant. Any time you can find a shaded shoreline or even a large boulder that casts a shadow, toss a topwater. The topwater bite can be good at any time of the day, but is especially strong in the late afternoon when water temperatures are often at their warmest.

Cold Front/Crawfish Pattern

I used the cold front/crawfish pattern late one October on a trip to West Virginia's New River. When I arrived, I saw a trio of challenging circumstances facing me. First, I found from talking with local anglers that the air temperature had dropped from the mid-60s to the lower 50s over the course of several days—a precipitous drop to be sure. Second, a cold front had come marauding through the area, leaving a bluebird sky and, of course, plunging water temperatures. And, third, because of prior commitments, I would only be able to ply the New from 10 a.m. until 2 p.m., not exactly prime time during an autumn cold front.

I quickly decided that the topwater bite would be non-existent and that given the smallies' benumbed states, they would not likely show an inclination to charge after rapidly retrieved crankbaits or spinnerbaits, streamers or nymphs. It was time for some "grind it out" fishing.

On smallmouth rivers, that often means methodically dragging 4-inch tubebaits or crayfish patterns a few inches at a time across the substrate. This tactic is slow, painstaking fishing in which you are likely to receive only a bite or two per hour. What's more, the bites you do come by will be very light, feathery affairs.

Employing this pattern, I was able to land several nice smallmouths, which to me was a real thrill given the terrible conditions. And all of those smallmouths were holding well out of the main current and also below current breaks such as boulders and submerged logs. Come autumn, cold

America's premier smallmouth rivers often flaunt Class I to III rapids, swiftly flowing water that can cause problems for novice river runners. If you are on your maiden river voyage, be sure to go with a veteran boater or an outfitter. Come fall, many rivers can rise suddenly, so you also should check U.S. Geological Survey Internet sites for current stream conditions.

And no matter what your boating skills, always wear a lifejacket the entire time you are in a craft. This is especially true in the fall when the cooler water temperatures can quickly cause hypothermia.

front enduring bass will be well out of the main flow. They are not likely to move far or fast to hit a fly or lure.

Last, for larger bass, use the size 4 crayfish patterns or 3½ to 4-inch tubes that many companies now tie or make. Some of my most productive tubes have been Venom's Erie Series and Strike King's Kevin Van Dam Pro Models while the Clouser Crayfish is an obvious choice.

Chase Mode Smallmouths/Crankbait/Streamer Pattern

The chase mode smallmouths/crankbait/streamer pattern is the classic autumn smallmouth game plan and is also, perhaps, the one that outdoor writers most like to extol in print. Unfortunately, this gambit is also the most fickle of all fall patterns and also the most evanescent, often as brief as the so-called Indian Summer period.

When river smallmouths will track down a crankbait or streamer, you are assured of some of the most fetching fall action possible. The bass are aggressive; they will come long distances to hit a lure or fly, and no crank or streamer can be retrieved too quickly for their tastes. Outdoor scribes often write that smallmouths are in this mode throughout much of the fall, but in reality, the fish only act this belligerently for a very short period.

This period of scintillating action often occurs about two to three weeks after the weather has noticeably cooled from summer but before late autumn cold fronts begin to slam a river with regularity. In other words, the crankbait/streamer pattern is good for about a week to ten days; if you do not have the good fortune to be on the water during that span, you miss this bite entirely.

Crankbait/streamer chasing bass will hold in many areas. One of the best is an eddy or backwater. These areas where the current reverses upon itself draw active bass throughout the year, and the Indian Summer period is no exception. Smallmouths will also congregate along the main channel where they will be moving in and out from behind boulders and ledges.

Regardless of where these bass hold, the target of their desires is often baitfish. Those into colors (and as readers no doubt know by now, generally I am not) could include those that mimic shad, minnows, and small sunfish. Sound streamer choices include Shenk's White Streamers, Clouser's Deep Minnow line of streamers, and Zonkers. Effective lure choices include Storm Flat Warts, Bomber Model As, Rapala Shad Raps, and Bill Dance's Fat Free Shad series. Again, however, don't expect this bite to be long lasting.

Stained Water/Spinnerbait Pattern

The stained water/spinnerbait pattern often occurs late in autumn after a goodly amount of rainfall has taken place. This rain causes the leaves remaining on trees to fall in the water, making topwater offerings and crankbaits/streamers ineffective and constantly entangled with flotsam. This precipitation also results in a waterway becoming progressively more stained and the water temperature to descend into the low 50s.

Given all these circumstances, a spinnerbait becomes the logical choice. Chris Ellis, a former guide who now operates an advertising agency in Fayetteville, West Virginia, offers several tips.

"The stained water/spinnerbait pattern can be a real big bass one in late fall," said Ellis. "I prefer a ¼-ounce spinnerbait with a single Colorado blade and a chartreuse skirt. The Colorado blade gives me the thumping rhythm that I need, while the single blade setup is best for keeping the bait down near the bottom. And the chartreuse skirt offers more visibility in the discolored water.

"I like to slow roll the spinnerbait across the bottom, but I do change up a little bit. Most of the time, I will retrieve the bait so that it just ticks along across the bottom. But sometimes I will bring the bait off the bottom a few inches and let it fall backwards until the lure touches down. Then I will give the spinnerbait a quick, short little burst to make the blades start turning. That's when I often receive a strike."

Ellis relates that the stained water/spinnerbait pattern is most likely to occur in areas far removed from current. The more the water temperature drops, the more the various species of baitfish leave the areas where the water flows swiftest. And, of course, the smallmouths follow the forage.

Instead of checking out riffles, runs, and eddies, expect the smallmouths to locate in the deeper, slower-moving pools. The bass will often linger in those deeper holes that provide wood or rock cover. Ellis concludes by emphasizing that these bass often congregate by size now. Indeed, if you catch a hefty bronzeback on your first cast to one of these deep-water sanctuaries, you may be on your way to an impressive outing.

Full confession...I have no idea how to catch smallmouths on a fly rod when the water temperature has plunged, the water has become stained, and floating leaves cover the water. I know of no lure or fly, other than possibly the spinnerbait, that will really penetrate this mat of leaves and catch river smallmouths.

Transition Bass/Jig and Pig Pattern

The transition bass/jig and pig/crawfish pattern often comes into play when summer turns to autumn and when fall morphs into winter. These are times when the water temperature drops noticeably, often from the low 70s to the 60s in the former situation and from the low 50s to the 40s in the latter.

When these conditions take place, river smallmouths typically become inclined not to chase fast moving lures or flies, but they still sense the need to feed. A jig and pig or crayfish pattern is an ideal choice as either one offers a hearty mouthful for a sluggish smallie, but neither requires a great deal of energy to overtake.

One of the interesting inclinations of die-hard river smallmouth enthusiasts is their preference for hair jigs and flies. Many of the best anglers that I have met over the years tie their own with deer hair, although I once met an angler who preferred bear. And these spin fishermen as a group seem to fancy soft plastic trailers over the traditional pork ones.

Marty Shaffner, who operates Tri State Anglers Guide Services, ties a fly fishing version of the jig and pig, which he, of course, calls a jig and pig fly. Marty gave me one of these flies and it is indeed a work of art. Silicon rubber legs extend from the pattern's head, which is weighted with lead eyes, and a shammy tail adds verisimilitude. The body itself is very leech-like in shape and hackle. This is a go-to fly when smallmouths are deep and feeding on crayfish.

Knowing the best fall lures and flies can put anglers in a position to succeed come autumn.

But whatever their penchants for jig and trailer and crayfish material, I have noticed that these anglers are all very precise about how they retrieve their baits and flies. Typically, they hold the rod tips very high so as to keep in better contact with the baits. Second, these individuals painstakingly crawl their jig and pigs and crayfish patterns along the substrate, but at the same time they never allow these lures or flies to totally stop, realizing that to do so would invite a snag. And, last, these expert anglers set the hook hard at the faintest suggestion of a strike.

Regarding jig size, I have noticed a distinct seasonal bias. For example, when the summer to fall transition is underway, many anglers opt for the ⅛- or ¼-ounce sizes, given the low clear water that is typical then. Look for the bronzebacks to hold behind current breaks and in eddies, but also, and especially, in deep-water ledges.

During the fall to winter transition, these same sportsmen often go with heavier jigs from ⅜ to ½-ounce, given the stained water that is now the norm. This is also when the smallies will have moved to those deep-water hangouts detailed in the stained water/spinnerbait pattern.

Fly fishermen tend to opt for sizes 4, 6, and 8 patterns, but I have not noticed any difference in size choices based on the stage of the season.

Marty's jig and pig fly is a size 2/0, and, not surprisingly, he rarely catches small fish on it.

America's smallmouth rivers don't receive the fishing pressure that the nation's lakes do at any time of the year, and this is especially true during the fall. Use the patterns discussed here to score this autumn on a waterway near you.

Chapter 22

*T*he Truth about Fall Fishing
for River Smallmouths

The advent of autumn brings lower water temperatures and, consequently, river smallmouths "go on feeding binges" in order "to put on weight for the winter." Or so goes the conventional wisdom among many stream brown bass aficionados. Here is another old saying about moving water mossbacks: river bass "school up come fall" in order to prey more effectively upon the diminishing schools of minnows.

Are these commonly held beliefs fact or fiction? And regardless, just what are the major phases that smallmouths go through at the end of summer and then during the farewell to fall and the coming of winter? The Virginia Department of Game and Inland Fisheries biologist most responsible for keeping up with river smallmouths is Scott Smith. I asked him to help us better understand smallmouth behavior come autumn.

During the Fall, Do River Smallmouths Feed More Heavily in Preparation for Winter?

"I think the fish probably do feed a little more in early fall—at least during the day—when the water first starts to cool off," said Smith. "I don't know if anyone has ever figured out if the fish feed to put on weight for the winter, but anything is possible. Since their metabolic rates are controlled by temperature—one of the hazards of being cold blooded—that probably has as much to do with it as anything. My guess is that anglers perceive an increase in smallmouth feeding because the fish are more active during the middle of the day when most of the anglers are out."

In the summer, river brown bass often feed at night and during low light conditions such as dawn and dusk—times when few anglers are on the water to notice that behavior. As Smith states, more anglers notice bass feeding in the fall because the fish are more visible doing so. And as far as the old axiom about fish trying to put on weight for the winter, aren't all species of fish (and for that matter, all predators) always instinctively trying to feed and put on weight? That's what predators do—prey.

In Fall, Do Bass Form Schools to More Efficiently Attack Prey?

"I know that at certain times of the year (that is, at other times besides fall) smallmouths do form loose groups, but not really a tight school like you see with minnows or shad," said Smith. "I've also seen that when the water becomes really cold—below 50 degrees—the larger fish seem to be grouped together. This may be where this myth originates."

The truth here, then, is that river smallmouths are likely to form "loose" schools as Smith states, when feeding conditions or circumstances warrant, regardless of the season. For example, one July day on a tributary of the James River, I observed a "school" of four good-sized smallmouths that had banded together to attack a small water snake that was desperately fleeing across the creek. The bass were so intent on their prey that when the snake finally slithered upon the shore, one of the smallies leaped part way upon the bank in one last desperate attempt to engulf the reptile. That incident was a "feeding frenzy" if I ever saw one. After the snake escaped, school was out, and the smallmouths went their separate ways.

Smith's statement about smallmouths grouping together by size when the water temperature drops below 50 is a known fact. But this phenomenon typically occurs in the winter months and is a major reason why cold water anglers often do extremely well—or very poorly. The bigger smallmouths hold only in a few areas—often specific places in deep, rocky pools—and fishermen either find these places or do not.

The Stages of Autumn: The Low Clear Water of Early Fall

Alec Burnett is a California fishing addict and former guide. Although he fishes with both spinning and fly fishing gear, he says the latter is often his choice in early fall—mid-September to mid-October—when the water is typically low, clear, and still warm.

"The gentle presentation that a fly rod can offer is often the way to go then," said Burnett. "In early fall, the water is usually as clear and as low as it will be all year, so being able to drop a fly down on the surface from a long way off and with a minimum of disturbance is key. The conditions are also why the best time to fish is typically very early and late in the day under low light."

Blane Chocklett, shown here with some of his favorite fall flies, believes that fall can be an excellent time to catch river smallmouths, as long as the angler has some basic knowledge.

For this topwater action, Burnett prefers topwater patterns such as Walt's or Bob's Poppers (in sizes 2 to 6) and damsel flies in sizes 6 and 8. The guide will also opt for a Crease fly, a foam body popper that is effective "when you don't want the big bloop." He admits that he does not like to fish during the middle of the day in early fall, but if he has to, he looks for deep-water ledges or seams and pockets below rapids.

"Strip a Woolly Bugger or a Muddler Minnow through deep water or where current exists," instructed Burnett. "Experiment with different size patterns and the speed of the retrieve. Use a sink tip leader or split shot to force a fly to descend as deep as possible."

The Cold Fronts of October

Blane Chocklett guides on the James and New, and he operates Blue Ridge Fly Fishers, (540) 563-1616, in Roanoke, Virginia. Chocklett freely admits that an October cold front will leave the fish turned off and make fishing extremely difficult.

"Usually, when an October cold front hits an area, I try to fish the middle of the day," he explained. "That's when the fish will be most active, relatively speaking. My goal is to fish slower and deeper and to be very patient and work an area hard before leaving it. Frankly, the cold temperatures and blue skies of an October cold front are a lot more typical than those instances when the fish are going on those 'feeding frenzies' that outdoor writers are always writing about."

Along with the slower and deeper presentation, the Roanoke guide narrows his focus to just two locales: deep-water ledges and drop-offs. He probes those places with size 2 and 4 crayfish patterns and two patterns that he has created: the size 2 Chocklett Sculpin and the similarly sized Chocklett Disc Minnow. All these flies are deployed on sink tip lines.

"Even though you will be fishing primarily along the bottom in deep pools, you still should be very careful with your casts," concluded Chocklett. "I stay well away from target areas and either make long casts from my drift boat or get out and wade. The fish are hard enough to catch without spooking them with sloppy casts or careless wading."

The Plunging Temperatures of November

Just when anglers think that the October cold fronts will be the worst thing they have to contend with, along comes early November and, quite typically, rapidly decreasing water temperatures. Those cold, daylong rains that often arrive in early November can easily cause the water temperature to descend from the upper 50s into the upper 40s over the course of a fortnight.

Normally when stream smallmouth fishing in the spring, summer, and fall, I bring along four rods and a wide assortment of lures and flies. But when the water temperature plummets, I drastically reduce my arsenal. I primarily rely on a single baitcaster, a 6½-foot medium heavy Quantum Tour Edition, and a reel spooled with 10-pound-test Trilene XL.

Bait choice is similarly constricted. The only two baits I rely on are 6-inch Mister Twister Phenom worms and 4-inch Venom tubes. The smallies are not going to be moving far or fast to engulf a bait, and I want lures, like these soft plastic offerings, that can be inched along the bottom and, at times, left motionless for long intervals. To prevent snags, I Texas-rig the worms and tubes. To keep them on the bottom, I use sliding bullet sinkers, usually the ¼-ounce size.

One fall rule that I strongly believe in is that the colder the water temperature, the more river smallmouths shy away from current. No longer do I look for fish in the push water above a rapid or in the swift water below. Instead, I seek out side eddies, that is, eddies adjacent to the faster water below a rapid. These eddies must contain laydowns or large rocks in order to draw brown bass.

I am not going to pretend that I experience "fall feeding frenzies." On a recent trip to the New River during this period, I caught only two smallies, a 12- and a 15-incher, which fell for tubes dragged through eddies. And I went home feeling very good about my day on the water.

Late Fall: More Challenges

Barry Loupe is a former guide on the New and North Fork of the Holston. The Saltville, Virginia, resident says the biggest challenge of late fall—when the water temperature has permanently dropped below 50 degrees—is understanding where the fish congregate.

"At this time, smallmouths typically move to slack water areas near current but protected from it," said Loupe. "Good places to look for bass are deep-water ledges, logjams, large boulders, and sandbars. These areas provide cover and, if crawfish and baitfish are also present, they may draw bass. I emphasize the word *may*. Smallmouths tend to congregate by size now in only a few places. One certain place may hold ten nice-sized smallmouths and five other very similar places may not hold a single fish.

"My method is 'low and slow' patient finesse fishing. Contrary to popular belief, smallmouths can become quite aggressive now, if the conditions are right, such as a three day warming trend that raises the temperature several degrees. The problem is, though, that even these 'active' fish may only feed once or twice in a day. What seems like a wasted day for six or so hours may quickly turn into an awesome display of smallmouth action … that lasts all of 15 or 30 minutes. Perseverance is key."

Loupe favors only a handful of baits now. Tubes, Case Magic Stiks, and ⅛-ounce Butch Neal handcrafted jigs tipped with Venom trailers are his go-to lures. He prefers a 6½-foot medium heavy rod with a Browning reel, spooled with 8-pound test.

I suppose the only definitive "facts" about fall river smallmouth fishing are that the season has many stages, the brown bass themselves undergo many moods, and the fishing can be very good or gosh awful. The next time some outdoor scribe waxes on about "fall feeding frenzies" and "smallies schooling up," take the writer's words with a grain of salt.

Chapter 23

Be a Contrarian Angler

When fishing, not many bass anglers bring along a book with the sayings of the great nineteenth century American essayist Ralph Waldo Emerson. Perhaps more of us should. For one of Emerson's most profound maxims is that "a foolish consistency is the hobgoblin of little minds." In twenty-first century English, the quote means that it pays in life (as it often does in fishing) to go against the grain, to be a contrarian, once in a while.

Be a Contrarian in Lure and Fly Selection

An experience on the James River near my Southwest Virginia home shows the folly of blindly trusting conventional wisdom. About five years ago on this water, soft plastic jerkbaits were all the rage, and the bass attacked them repeatedly. I remember talking to an angler who had caught some 90 bass on jerkbaits over the course of a day. Of course, I, like all the other locals, began casting very little other than these minnow imitations and scored well with them.

The next year, I noticed that the soft plastic jerkbait bite, though still strong, was not what it had been the first year. And the bite continued to progressively tail off over the course of the next two years. During the fifth year of the "soft plastic jerkbait era," I stopped throwing these bogus minnows at all and experienced an excellent topwater bite on other surface lures and flies throughout the warm water period.

Meanwhile during that fifth year, I noted that many anglers were still slavishly addicted to what had become the conventional wisdom:

soft plastic jerkbaits were the number one lure, surface or subsurface, on the James River. I even once came across a guide who was instructing his two clients to rig all their rods (each man had three) with varying sizes of soft plastic jerkbaits.

At the end of the day, I made it a point at the ramp to ask them how they had done. They had caught a few, they said, but the fish weren't really biting. My friend and I, employing a variety of offerings, had easily limited out. The truth is that soft plastic jerkbaits have become what every other bait or fly is—an offering that definitely has times and situations when it performs well, and times when it doesn't. Currently on my home body of water, soft plastic jerkbaits should be used, but not exclusively. I have no doubt that in another three or four years—when the masses have finally become disenchanted with soft plastic jerkbaits—that they will once again become a very productive bait. Bass do become wary of any offering when they are exposed to it constantly.

I strongly believe that it pays to be a contrarian in lure and fly selections. For example, one of my favorite strategies when visiting a river that I am unfamiliar with is to call a local tackle shop right before I travel to the area. I ask for the lowdown on the hot lures and flies— and then I make sure to use something else.

If, for example, the tackle shop proprietor says that his clients are all using alphabet-style crankbaits, then the first crankbait out of my box is a flat crank. And if a fly shop operator claims that poppers and chuggers are the way to go, then I rely on damsel and dragonfly patterns.

Another contrarian strategy is to employ lures or flies that are "out of style." For spin fishermen, these include such baits as 6-inch plastic worms, inline spinners, silver spoons, and floating-diving minnows. For fly fishermen, especially during the summer and fall months, the out of style patterns are nymphs. How many times do we see long rodders casting nymphs during the warm weather period? Yet, the anglers who do often catch nice smallies.

My good friend Rick Moorer regularly catches big bass on ⅛-ounce inline spinners from his home body of water. Whenever the bite becomes slow and fishing pressure intense, he conducts a milk run down a series of honey holes and absolutely wears the bass out on these little blade baits.

Quite frankly, I cannot understand why the bass hit my friend's spinners. Perhaps Emerson once again has the answer: "To be great is to be misunderstood." Great anglers often are contrarians.

Be a Contrarian in Locale Selection

I also believe that wise anglers are contrarians in locale selection. For example, on the James River, a "community hole" exists that for many years always held bass throughout the year. Almost everybody regularly made stops there, and the site almost always produced a nice brown bass or two.

However, about five years ago, some bank erosion occurred, and this community hole (which is a backwater just off the main channel) suffered some heavy sedimentation. The site now is a gathering ground for rough fish and nothing else. But every time I pass by this former hot spot, I observe a boat or two full of fishermen foolishly flinging away.

Two lessons come from this anecdote. The first is that river conditions change over the course of time. Keep informed about the evolution of your home waterway. And, second, never base your bassing game plan on visits to a series of local hot spots. Put together four or five different patterns per season, and make sure that each pattern includes a variety of locales that are likely to hold fish. Ideally, some of these patterns should include deep-

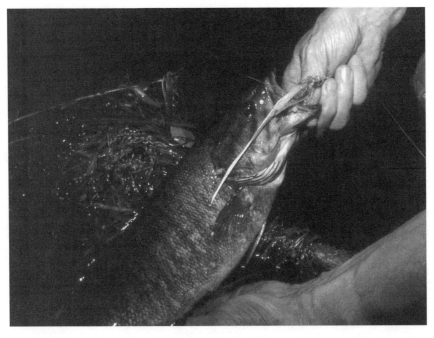

Being a contrarian angler—for example, using flies and lures and/or sizes that the bass don't often see—can lead to great success.

water bass sanctuaries (which are less visible and less heavily pressured) such as channel drop-offs and deep-water humps and ledges.

There are other ways to be a contrarian in locale selection. For example, most everyone fishes outside bends. But on your home river, journey directly across the stream to the inside bend and look for cover there. You likely will not find as many bass, but the ones available could be quite receptive to a fly or lure. A good friend and I do this at our favorite fishing locale but only when no other boat is visible. And we have caught numerous nice smallmouth bass on this inside bend.

Another underutilized place is the launch area where everyone puts in. For example, last year, I was asked to be an observer at a youth fishing rodeo. The youngsters were restricted to fishing around a ramp that is the most heavily used one on the river. County busybodies have removed all the trees from the shoreline; the result, I thought, was a barren wasteland.

Yet at the youth tournament, the winning child weighed in a 4-pound-plus smallmouth, and the second place tike landed a 3½-pounder. (This was after I told the promoter that the kids would be lucky to catch a sunfish.) The lesson I learned here is that all sorts of non-standard places can hold some fairly hefty bass—places that everyone ignores.

Another example of a similarly overlooked place is a swimming area. If your home river possesses a swimming area, check out the area "beyond the ropes." Chances are that the drop-off right past those ropes receives little fishing pressure. Emerson once more offers a nugget of wisdom: "I hope in these days we have heard the last of conformity and consistency." Don't conform to the conventional wisdom concerning where to fish.

Be a Contrarian in Time Selection

Like many anglers, I have a Monday through Friday job that keeps me off the water during most weekdays. If I launch on Saturday and Sunday mornings, I am competing with scores of other anglers. Thus, I have taken to sleeping in on weekends and not arriving at a river until around noon. This is a particularly good time to put in on Sundays when everyone has left off fishing to prepare for the workweek ahead. Fishing, not surprisingly, has been great, and fishing pressure (as well as that awful pleasure boating presence) has been quite light.

Other ways exist as well to be a contrarian in time selection. I know of two fisheries biologists who leave work at 4:30 p.m. on Tuesday afternoons in the summer and are on a nearby body of water by 5 p.m. They fish until 10 p.m. and experience several distinct fish activity periods: an evening bite, a twilight bite, and a real frenzy about 90 minutes after sundown. The catch rates of the two men have been phenomenal, and they rarely encounter other anglers.

Although fishing after dark during the summer months has become common on many major rivers, the after-sundown angler contingent still does not have as much competition for the bass as a daytime fisherman does. I also know of several anglers who have become enamored with fishing after dark during the spring and fall. Of course, the night air is much cooler then, but many nights the fishing is outstanding. The late evening bite, especially, can be quite good.

I also have done more winter bass fishing the past few years than I have ever done before. Little, if any, boating pressure exists at this time of year, and precious few anglers venture forth either. In fact, one of my best friends, Barry Loupe of Saltville, has become an expert at winter bass fishing and insists that the cold water period has become his favorite period for catching trophy mossybacks.

If you have no choice but to be on a river when the masses are, seek out places that other anglers shun. For example, one angler I know does well when fishing a warm water discharge during the heat of the summer. Another likes to cast to concrete walls that border waterfront property, reasoning that other "rock anglers" will be targeting riprap or rock piles. As Emerson states: "It is easy in the world to live after the world's opinion; it is easy in solitude to live after our own." Translated into fishing lingo, this maxim means that we can blindly fish where and when everyone else does, or we can be a contrarian and look for times and places when we will have relative solitude—and better fishing—on our home bodies of water.

Summing Up

All of Ralph Waldo Emerson's quotes for this story come from his timeless essay, "Self Reliance," in which he urges people to develop trust in themselves. All of us sportsmen should dare to trust our instincts, to become contrarian anglers, boldly marching to the beat of the proverbial different drummer. As Emerson maintains: "Whoso must be a man, must be a nonconformist." Merely substitute the word *angler* for *man*.

Part Five:
Winter Smallmouth Fishing

Chapter 24

$\mathcal{F}$ive Hot Spots for Late Fall/Early Winter
River Smallmouths

Come that infamous transition period between fall and winter, hardcore bass anglers who want to continue fishing know that they will be faced with some of the most difficult conditions of the year. However, these individuals know that before winter blankets the region, the bass do congregate in certain areas and do continue to feed—although obviously not as much or as often as they did earlier in the season. Here, then, are the last five places to check out before the smallmouths go deep for the duration.

Mouths of Spring-Fed Creeks

On my home body of water, one of the most reliable late fall locales is the mouth of a certain creek. But the main reason this tributary remains so productive year after year is because it is fed by a spring. Springs, regardless of where they exist, typically register a water temperature somewhere from the low to mid-50s. Even when the water temperature in a river has plunged below 45 degrees, for example, the area around the creek mouth will still be over 50 degrees.

The colder the air and water temperatures become in autumn, the more bass I find around this spring-fed creek. Indeed, if you can locate three or four of these types of tributaries on your home river, you can cobble together a milk run that can produce consistent limits. Although the warmer water alone will be enough to draw bass, my favorite spring-fed tributary performs well because it features a number of basketball-sized rocks at its mouth. The combination of warmer water and permanent, stable cover is simply unbeatable.

Regarding lures, the warmer water within these tributaries allows you to employ faster moving baits. While in other areas of the lake, you might have to resort to jig and pigs or plastic worms to score, spring-fed creeks allow you to work crankbaits and spinnerbaits.

Regarding flies, try Clouser Minnows and Crayfish, Clouser Deep Sculpins, and beadhead nymphs. Begin by rapidly stripping these patterns, but don't be surprised if you have to slow down your presentation.

Still-Living Grass Beds

Another superb situation during the fall/winter transition is a still-living grass bed. Black bass, like most predators, are creatures of the edge; that is, they like to hunt for prey where one habitat blends into another. Because of this transitional nature of grass beds, they attract smallmouth bass throughout the year. But aquatic growth becomes progressively more appealing as little by little, less and less of it exists.

One of the most important considerations to keep in mind when fishing a transitional period grass bed is how vibrant it is. Bass simply will not remain around a rapidly decaying grass bed, even if portions of it are still green and lush. So the grass bed that held bass one week might totally lack fish the next. You might even run a grass gathering offering, such as a crankbait or streamer, through a deep-water bed before committing to fishing it. If your choices come back with a gob of brown leaves, for example, you should probably leave immediately.

For underwater grass beds, a spinnerbait is one of the most reliable artificials. Just as you would in the summer and early fall, retrieve this bait just deeply enough so that you can feel the blades ticking over the surface of the growth. For surface mats or vegetation just below the water level, try plastic worms or craw worms. Pitch or flip them to any openings in the grass or anywhere the growth forms a point—no matter how small. Peg bullet sinkers so as to keep hang-ups to a minimum.

Similarly, long rodders can begin with a streamer on a weight forward floating line and then go to a sink tip one with weighted streamers and nymphs. This time of year would be a good one to bring along several fly rods.

Points that Run into the Main Channel

Surely one of the most consistent locales to fish during the transition period is a long, slowly tapering point that connects with the main channel. The reasons are many. First, no matter what the surface water temperature is, a bass can find a comfort zone somewhere along an extended point that features a number of different water depths.

Second, long points typically contain a variety of cover forms: wood, rocks, and grass, for example. If you determine that the pattern on one particular day is that the bass are feeding on crawfish and are orienting around wood in deep water, then you can concentrate on those points that are known to have wood cover. And you can catch them by tossing a jig and pig or weighted crayfish to those areas.

If the bass are chasing minnows along the bank, you will always find more bass on banks with points than you will on shorelines without these features. And spinnerbaits and streamers are obvious choices for such a situation. What's more, the colder the weather becomes or if a cold front crashes down on your home body of water, then you can re-locate to the deeper edges of a point. Concentrate, then, on where the point actually intersects with the main channel. Deep diving crankbaits and weighted nymphs are ideal for this type of situation.

Deep-Water Humps

One of the great aspects of deep-water humps during the changeover from autumn to winter is that they receive much less fishing pressure than spring-fed creeks, tapering points, and especially the easily recognizable, still-vibrant grass beds. This is true even though many anglers are adept today at finding humps with some hardcore river rats even using sonar. Still, the industrious angler can locate rises that other individuals have overlooked.

Another attribute of humps is that they create multiple edge areas. Don't perceive a hump to be like a cereal bowl, although that is the common understanding (or misunderstanding) of this bass-holding ground. Instead, visualize humps as multi-sided structures that have many uneven sides, periodic raised areas, and all kinds of rock and wood debris strewn on top of them and adjacent to those sides. Humps in shallower water may still have vegetation at this advanced stage of this season. Almost all of them have flotsam such as sunken driftwood, old logs, and maybe even trees that once sank during a flood.

Most of the time, I have found the most active fish to be on the top of the hump. Then, a good tactic to take these fish is to slowly retrieve a streamer or a single Colorado blade spinnerbait across the structure.

A marvelous fall tactic is to Carolina-rig a lizard or a grub along the sides of humps, especially those that extend for considerable distances. And a deep running crankbait is yet another viable tool for this situation.

An added bonus of humps is that they remain attractive to bass no matter what the weather conditions are. As readers well know, the weather

Check out the hot spots detailed in this chapter to experience more later fall and early winter success.

in this region can be notoriously fickle this time of year. Expect more cool and windy days than sunny, fair ones. Regardless of the weather, though, humps will attract and retain smallies.

Logs Found Near Deep Water

Logs are some of the most recognizable, and most fished, forms of cover on rivers and creeks. In fact, many if not most logs pull in bass throughout the warm water period. But come the transition from fall to winter, smallies, especially the good-sized ones, typically leave those logs that rest in shallow water.

Now is the time to frequent those lay downs that have ends that either contact deeper water or offer ready access to the depths. In fact, many veteran anglers don't even bother to cast to the back ends (that is the section that touches the shoreline) at this time of year. They instead have located a dozen or so deep-water lay downs and exclusively fish only the tips of them.

Although the types of logs that attract smallmouth bass during the transition period are much different than the kinds that draw bass for much of the year, the approach to fishing this cover does not change. As is true most of the year, streamers and nymphs and plastic worms and jig and pigs remain outstanding options.

One autumn, a friend and I journeyed to a favorite fishing spot and encountered a bluebird sky, falling air temperatures, cold water, and lethargic bass. We concentrated on the types of areas mentioned in this story, using our canoe to run and gun from one habitat form to another. Although our success rate was not what it would have been had we been fishing during the pre-spawn, the post-spawn, or in early fall, we still enjoyed a successful outing, landing some nice bass.

I am not going to pretend that the fall/winter transition period is my favorite time to bass fish. It most definitely is not. But visiting the five types of places detailed here can result in some satisfying days on the water.

Chapter 25

Five Hot Spots for Late Winter/Early Spring
River Smallmouths

As late winter metamorphoses into early spring, again the old real estate truism—location, location, location—applies to smallmouth rivers. The number one reason we will or will not catch bass now is whether we have selected the right locations to fish.

Mud or Muck Flats

During the early season period, anglers often talk about the bass being in certain areas in preparation for the spawn. Actually, though, at this stage of the year, a bass is much more interested in finding the warmest water possible and obtaining a maximum amount of nourishment, while at the same time expending a minimum amount of energy.

That's why mud or muck flats can be so productive early in the fishing season. Dark-bottomed flats are known to retain heat better than light-colored ones, and bass definitely can sense minute differences in water temperature. A mud flat might have water that is only a degree or two warmer than a nearby sand flat, but to a bass still benumbed from a harsh winter, that small variation in temperature is very noticeable and attractive.

Of course, not just any mud or muck flat will possess warmer water and consequently pull in bass. For a bank to be productive, it must lie in full or at least partial sun for a good part of the day. If the shoreline surrounding the flat is heavily covered with evergreens such as pines, then the sun's warming rays will be blocked.

Also, if the flat lies in water that is deep relative to the overall depth and water clarity of the river, then the sun's rays will not be able to penetrate enough to warm the bottom.

If the above conditions are favorable, anglers will no little trouble ascertaining what the bass will be feeding on at a mud or muck flat—crayfish. I have caught bass that actually had muddy snouts from probing about in the substrate so much. All kinds of crayfish imitations will produce, both the fly and lure variety.

A standard choice is a size 2 weighed crawfish, as is a 3- or 4-inch crawdad attached to a Carolina rig. Given the snag free nature of mud and muck flats, Carolina-rigged crustaceans are excellent choices, and anglers will rarely have to worry about retying. Split shot rigs are similarly effective for both fly and spin fishermen, and the new drop shot getups on the market give the fish something they do not often see. Regardless of which rig or size crayfish you select, remember to retrieve your offerings at a very slow pace. Nature's mudbugs will not be moving very fast now and neither should yours.

Tributary Confluences

Where a tributary enters also draws bass during the early season period. But just as with mud or muck flats, these creeks must possess specific qualities. The most important of these traits is that some form of cover must be present. If summer cabins or all-season homes lie along these mini-waterways, the owners may have placed riprap around the bank and unwittingly provided excellent cover for the bass.

Another virtue of riprap is that probably no other form of cover is as good at retaining heat. A 20-yard-long section of riprap, if it has been blessed to receive Old Sol's emanations even for an hour or two a day, may have water as much as two or three degrees warmer than surrounding areas. And, again, that small variation in temperature is extremely important this early in the year.

Shoreline rocks and boulders can be just as inviting to heat-seeking bass. In fact, if these rocks are scattered and/or few in number, they may be even more productive than riprap. A savvy angler can put together a rock pattern and travel from bank to bank, meanwhile fishing nothing else. The bass simply have to be on these isolated rocks, and they will likely be holding on the downstream sides of this cover. Conversely, we know for sure that bass will be holding on a riprapped bank, but with such an abundance of cover in one location, finding the fish can be more challenging.

Wood is another excellent form of cover to check out at confluences. At this time of year, I generally prefer elongated logs that have their bases attached to the bank. There is no telling just where a bass will be holding on these downed trees, but a tree that extends from shallow to deep water will likely have a fish occupying it somewhere along its length. The same cannot always be said about, say, a log that is parallel to the shoreline and lying in several feet of water.

Marty Shaffner, who operates Tri-State Angler Guide Service, opts for several fly patterns. One is his jig and pig fly (discussed earlier) and a second is a size 2 weighed nymph.

"For wood and rocks, I like to fish either an unweighted fly with a sink tip line or a weighed fly with a regular line," said Shaffner. "Both of these outfits have the ability to get down fast but not get hung up."

By far, my best lure for early season tributary fishing has been a 3-inch grub. The grub should be threaded onto a jighead so that the hook is totally exposed. Early season bass are notorious for their light striking, and the exposed hook of these smallish lures is a real aid to increasing hookups. Retrieve this bait just fast enough so that it remains off the bottom.

Another effective lure for tributaries is a 3- to 6-inch suspending jerkbait, also in a minnow or baitfish pattern. During an early season foray last year, a friend of mine out fished me 5-to-1 while primarily employing suspending jerkbaits. The hovering ability of these bogus minnows can be a real turn-on to turned-off bass. At this time of year, don't retrieve this lure in wide sweeping jerks. Merely crank it down to the desired depth, maintain a steady retrieve, and periodically cease the return for several seconds or so.

Main Channel Drop-Offs

Main channel drop-offs are a known big bass hangout now. And for years, knowledgeable anglers have been aware of that fact, although still too many anglers continue to pound away at the banks.

That may be true because it is so easy to go down a bank and fish visible cover. But if you are trying to catch some real kicker bass, start your search along the main channel. Big bass have a true affinity for channel drop-offs. The environment is stable there, the current is not pronounced, food exists in sufficient amounts, and, as noted, angling pressure is extremely light—especially during the late winter/early spring period.

The number of feet required to make a main channel drop-off a prime one is really a matter of the physical nature of your home river. If you primarily ply a shallow stream, a depth change of as little as a foot can be extremely significant. If your river is a major one, a 3- to 5-foot drop (or more) may be required before the bass will claim it as their own.

The importance of the size of the drop-off is yet another reason why few anglers fish this form of structure. Hunting for these areas and determining their bass potential is just as important as knowing how to fish them properly.

Unfortunately, anglers who commit to finding and fishing main channel drop-offs at this time of year are not guaranteed success. Of the five bass holding areas listed here, I would rate this locale as by far the most difficult one to work a bait or fly along. Perhaps the best options are a jig and pig, Marty Shaffner's jig and pig fly, or a Carolina-rigged lizard.

In order to maintain bottom contact and a better feel for the bottom, heavier jigs in the ½-ounce and above sizes are preferred, as are 2/0 flies. Jigs and jig flies offer excellent depth and speed control, and today's highly advanced rods proffer excellent feel. The ability to detect the slightest pickup of a bait or fly is crucial, given the light-striking nature of bass now.

Carolina-rigged lizards bring the same positives as jig and pigs do and are less likely to snag on the bottom. The best drop-offs often have some kind of cover on them, and the combination of structure (a main channel drop-off) and cover (rock or wood) is the ideal situation at any time of the year.

As winter gives way to early spring, a deep water bank drenched in sunshine can be a marvelous place for anglers to look for stream smallies.

Points with Pronounced Drops

Whereas few anglers will bother to explore main channel drop-offs, many of us do recognize the need to investigate points, which are much easier to locate and travel along. All kinds of points exist on rivers: those with gentle declinations, gradual slopes, and pronounced drop-offs. The last category is the one we should home in on during the early season.

This is because smallmouth bass are extremely sluggish at this time of year and really do not have the energy to expend to travel widely for food. A pronounced drop-off gives the bass several advantages. First, if a fish's instincts determine that conditions are favorable for a brief period of foraging, the bass can rise up from the bottom of a drop-off to its lip. This move is often only of a few feet and little energy is lost.

When the brief flurry of activity concludes or weather conditions become unfavorable, a bass can merely settle down to its previous depth. This economy of motion is critical to a bass' survival. Over the years, I have had many biologists tell me that 30 to 50 percent of any given year's class of bass do not survive from one year to the next. And the most common reason for bass mortality is winter die-off, another good reason why bass try to waste as little energy as possible in late winter.

As is true on main channel drop-offs, any little snippet of cover on point drop-offs is very significant. Points, especially if they are located on outside bends, often tend to be repositories for numerous kinds of wood, both of the human-made and natural variety.

A marvelous artificial for points is a ⅜ to ⅝ spinnerbait with a single Colorado blade. A Colorado-bladed bait will quickly helicopter down to the bottom; and given its lack of lift, this kind of spinnerbait maintains good contact with the substrate. Obviously, the technique to employ is slow rolling. With a minimum of practice, anglers will be able to walk a spinnerbait along the bottom, up to the lip, and then down the drop-off itself.

A crankbait is another excellent choice for point probing, but make sure you have a very slow gear ratio. The last thing you want is for your crankbait to be going much faster than the proverbial snail's pace. Paired with this reel should be light line. Of course, on some rivers, depending on cover, light line may be defined quite differently. Light line is needed though because it enables a bait to dive deeper and to remain closer to the bottom. This is a very important consideration for early season angling on points.

Marty Shaffner bluntly assesses a fly fisherman's ability to work a point or any deep water structure or cover now.

"Deep water smallmouths are really hard for fly fishermen to catch now," he told me. "Size 2/0 to size 2 Woolly Buggers drifted next to the bottom will work, but fishing them is a really tough deal. But if you are a die-hard fly fisherman, try the Bugger and stick with it. Eventually this pattern will pay off for you."

Deep-Water Banks

Of the quintet discussed here, deep-water banks are a favorite of many anglers. They have the advantage of being easy to find, and they are just as easy to work. And because most rivers receive little pressure at this stage of the fishing season, you will have little competition for these bass. Of course, the best deep-water banks lie in full sun for part of the day, and they should also harbor some kind of rock and/or wood cover.

Another situation to look for is a bank where the main channel swings in close to the shoreline. On many rivers, the reason why deep water exists along the bank is because the main channel is adjacent to it. A log that extends out to the edge of a channel can provide simply marvelous fishing now.

My favorite bait is one that few anglers use at this time of year: the venerable plastic worm. Although many anglers consider bogus annelids to be warm weather artificials, they have been among my most productive baits now.

One year, for example, on a cold windy day with a bluebird sky, I launched my Dagger Legend canoe for the first time that year. My first stop was a deep-water bank that had both rock and wood along the bottom. My third cast with a 6-inch, Texas-rigged black plastic worm produced the first smallmouth bass of the year—a chunky two-pounder. Forget the old saw that the water temperature has to be at a certain level for worms to be productive; they will entice fish right now.

If plastic worms fail to produce results, switch to 6-inch, Texas-rigged lizards. Sometimes the additional action that is inherent in a lizard is all that is needed to awaken a sluggish smallie. For either the imitation worm or salamander, use the lightest bullet sinker that you can get away with and still maintain contact with the bottom. A slow fall is best along deep-water banks. And as was true on point drop-offs, slow speed baitcasting reels are the correct choice.

Marty Shaffner recommends size 1/0 sculpins for this situation, but again emphasizes that plying these patterns is an arduous undertaking for long rodders. However, he notes that sculpins can produce quality sized off-season smallies, as well.

Regardless of where you fish now, keep these points in mind. First, fishing will be better if the water temperature has risen for several days in a row, no matter how low it was to start with. A rising temperature is almost always better than a reading that is higher but decreasing.

Second, afternoon action is almost always better than the morning bite. And the peak fishing often takes place during the last 90 minutes of daylight. Third, don't wait for the weekend to go fishing; head for the river if the weather conditions are favorable—rising temperature, sunny afternoon, and a stable weather pattern. I have a friend who keeps his fishing gear in his car at this time of the year. If the weather is promising when he leaves work at 3 p.m., he heads for a nearby river and fishes from the shore. This buddy often catches more fish than others do while fishing from a boat during a weekend when the conditions are less favorable.

Mud or muck flats, tributary entrances, main channel drop-offs, points with pronounced drops, and deep-water banks are five important places for the early season river basser to key in on. Don't expect the sizzling action you might enjoy in just a month or two. But do expect to catch your first quality bronzebacks of the year.

Chapter 26

How to Catch "Neutral" River Smallmouths

A real pet peeve of mine concerning bass fishing is when I hear anglers claiming to be experts at catching inactive fish. I'm not sure if I have ever caught an inactive bass—and I would wager that is true for the majority of America's anglers. Jim Ayres, who operates Gone Fishin', (888) 470-3131, in Oak Hill, West Virginia, regularly guides for largemouths, smallmouths, and spots on the entire gamut of bass habitats: lowland lakes, upland reservoirs, lowland waterways, and highland rivers.

"There are ways to catch inactive bass, but it is a rare occasion that you can do so," said Ayres. "There are probably only a handful of people who can actually catch fish that have truly shut down. By definition, an inactive bass is one that is lying dormant, is not hungry, not aggressive, and basically is in a resting state."

Ayres maintains that a tournament or recreational angler who encounters inactive bass would be better off leaving the area in order to look for neutral or active bass elsewhere instead of deciding to stay put and endeavoring to "make" those fish bite. This belief runs counter to the conventional wisdom proverb that "anglers should never leave fish to look for fish." The guide offers these definitions for neutral and active bass.

"A neutral bass is not necessarily dormant, it is probably semi-active, and it is definitely not aggressive," said Ayres. "In the spring, fishermen are most likely to find neutral bass right after the end of winter but before the pre-spawn period. The bass are starting to stage near the spawning areas, but they have not fully committed to moving shallow. And at the onset of a cold front, these fish will move right back deep again and suspend.

Most anglers can catch active river smallmouths; read here to catch those fish in a neutral mode.

"In the spring, an active bass is one that is in the pre-spawn mode, is hungry and gorging on crayfish, baitfish, or whatever the main forage species are, and is preparing to move shallow on to spawning areas but has not yet done so. In this type of situation, just about all retrieves and all categories of lures and flies work. This is the time and type of bass that an angler should use the kind of bait or fly that he knows how to work the best and has the most confidence in."

Spring Tactics for Catching Neutral Bass

Frankly, declares Jim Ayres, even individuals with limited skills should be able to boat satisfactory numbers of active bass during the spring months. But only highly knowledgeable anglers can outwit good numbers of neutral bass. During the spring, river smallmouths congregate in two main areas emphasizes Marty Shaffner, who operates Tri-State Angler Guide Service in North Carolina.

The first is a deep-water bank replete with rock and wood cover. This type of bank will produce even more quality smallmouths if trees extend out over the water. For this situation, Shaffner suggests drifting a size 2-6 Woolly Bugger under a strike indicator. Now, placing a Bugger under that canopy can be a challenge but the guide has a solution.

"The roll cast is a great way to shoot a fly under a tree canopy or under any other kind of overhanging cover as well," Shaffner told me. "But to really get the fly well back under the cover and tight to the bank and to keep far enough away that you don't spook the fish, you've got to put some snap to that roll cast.

"To do that, when you are on your back swing, stop the rod tip at two o'clock. Then push the rod forward with a hard snap at the end."

On one trip, Marty tutored me on how to accomplish what he calls the "snap roll cast" and I was able to add three or so feet to every cast. Those extra feet are a huge help in our being able to stay further away from the fish, yet place our fly patterns where they need to go. This is true not only in the spring but throughout the year.

Spin fishermen can work this type of area by slow rolling ⅜-ounce double willowleaf spinnerbaits. Retrieve this blade bait just fast enough that the lure ticks the bottom as it slowly moves just above the substrate.

A second place where neutral bass will assemble during the spring is a point out from the bank. Like lake bass, river smallies will move up and down the point depending on activity level. When they are in a neutral mode, of course, the fish will likely be deeper and farther away from the shoreline.

Shaffner lists Deep Clousers and what he calls "Half and Halves" (flies that are one-half Clouser Minnows and one-half Left Deceivers) as excellent pattern for this situation. Work the patterns shallow to deep, inching them along. Spinnerbaits are good choices for spin fishermen as are 4-inch soft plastic jerkbaits and ⅜-ounce jig and pigs.

The advantage of a soft plastic jerkbait is that it can be kept in the strike zone for such a long period of time. In the spring, too many spin fishermen work soft plastic jerkbaits too fast and too far above the bass,

Tips for Catching Inactive Bass

One of the best anglers I have ever fished with is Dave Maurice, who operates Venom Lures in Ohio, (800) 446-7510. As such, he often has to fish during the worst conditions that spring has to offer: plunging temperatures and barometers, as well as high winds.

"The best advice I can give for catching inactive fish is to not even bother to fool with those fish that have been moving back and forth from shallow to deep and then when they become inactive, end up suspending somewhere," says Maurice. "Those bass are the worst kind of inactive fish, and I can't catch them."

However, there is a small percentage of bass that always remain shallow and in a neutral state, even when conditions become terrible and most fish become inactive. Those are the fish that Maurice will target, and they will be holding along shallow banks and points. Come spring, like many anglers, Maurice likes to pitch rubber or silicon ¼- to ½-ounce jig and pigs for neutral bass. But for these shallow, inactive fish, he downsizes to ¼-ounce Venom hair jigs with 4-inch Venom Reefers (that have been cut in two) as trailers. To increase this bait's appeal, he inserts a 3mm glass rattle into the trailer.

The advantage a ¼-ounce hair jig has over a ¼-ounce regular jig, the Buckeye State sportsman explains, is that the former looks appreciably smaller than the latter—a crucial consideration when an angler needs his lure to maintain contact with the bottom but the bass are not inclined to want big mouthfuls.

Another favorite lure is a Venom Super Do (a type of drop bait) with a matching Super Do head of ¼- or ⅛-ounce. The entire length of this bait is only 3½ inches, and, as Maurice explained, "When an inactive bass picks up this bait, he's got it." For both the hair jig and the Super Do, slow retrieves with plenty of pauses prove most effective.

as well. In fact, fly fishermen are often guilty of the same haste. The result is that oftentimes the fish don't even realize that something to eat has entered their area. Crawl the jig and pig along the substrate, frequently pausing the retrieve for as long as ten seconds or longer.

Precious few anglers have learned how to actually catch inactive bass. And I would speculate that only a few of those anglers can consistently fool totally turned-off fish. The real geniuses of the bass fishing universe are those individuals who can regularly catch neutral bass—especially in the spring.

Chapter 27

All About Wood Cover

Learning how bass relate to wood and how to fish this form of cover are essential aspects of our sport. Here, then, are the major forms of human-made and natural wood cover and how to fish them.

Docks

At first thought, many river smallmouth anglers probably would say that on their home waters, docks are not major forms of cover, which is true. But just about every river that I have ever fished has a few docks along the shoreline over the course of the stream's length, and these few structures can be smallmouth magnets. The most important thing for anglers to keep in mind for this type of cover is that bass activity levels dictate their positioning. If the fish are active, look for them to be at the ends of these structures or just behind posts, facing outward, and willing to chase down fast moving baits/flies such as streamers, crankbaits, spinnerbaits, and buzzbaits. If the fish are not aggressive, present your offerings farther back under the cover and switch to Woolly Buggers, poppers, plastic worms, and jig and pigs.

Solid Debris

One of my favorite places to fish on the James River is a pool near a railroad track where a train once derailed and sent a load of wooden crossbars into the deep. We can't depend on train wrecks to commonly create cover, but we can count on our fellow humans to dump all manners of wood—planks, posts, housing construction material, for example—into bodies of water.

Given the random nature of how this debris descends into the depths, anglers should present their flies and baits from a variety of angles. Don't be afraid to run a crankbait like a Worden's Timber Tiger or a streamer like a Clouser through this cover.

Flotsam

Basically, flotsam is floating chunks, slivers, and random pieces of woody debris that have come to rest in eddies or in shoreline cuts. Flotsam in cuts looks promising, but usually is only productive when the main channel sweeps in tight to the shoreline. Flotsam in eddies is another story. Swimming a grub or ringworm on a jighead around outside edges of the eddy is an excellent tactic, as is stripping a Clouser or crayfish pattern. Spinnerbaits worked parallel to the sides can also produce, and poppers and chuggers are marvelous summertime patterns. Remember that bass found in eddies are there to feed and that they are willing to dash out from under flotsam to smash a lure.

Know Your Trees

I have always believed that anglers and hunters can experience more success if they know more about their environment, or as old timers called it, "practiced woodsmanship." A basic knowledge of which kinds of trees grow near water and whether these trees in their horizontal states are preferred or not by bass is, I believe, essential knowledge.

For instance, the American sycamore possesses many traits that make it a smallmouth bass magnet; this tree is a hardwood and has an enlarged base and numerous crooked branches. Sycamores thrive near water and are prime candidates to periodically topple into a river. When sycamore roots are exposed by wave action, they often become bass sanctuaries. Conversely, pine-covered river banks infrequently hold smallmouths; I have no idea why but it is true. For more information on trees and their traits, consult a field guide such as the Peterson's *Field Guide to Trees* or the Audubon Society's *Field Guide to North American Trees*.

Wood cover, such as this partially submerged log, can be a popular gathering place for river smallmouths.

Downed Trees

On the James River near my home, I can probe downed trees throughout the year and catch keeper sized and larger bass. That's because those trees possess two vital traits: they are hardwoods and they lie in deep water. Place a soft wood like pine or poplar in the same places as these trees lie, and they will hold fewer fish; they seem to be repelled by the rapid decomposition of soft wood under water. And any kind of laydown in thin water is often only a consistent producer in the spring. Once the water temperature warms into the 60s, buzzbaits and streamers are dynamite baits/flies to work across downed trees, but especially those that are still attached to banks.

Beaver Huts

In recent years, beavers have rapidly increased in number and are now regular denizens of rivers. I don't care for the destructive nature of these rodents, but I surely don't mind checking out their watery handiwork. Beavers often construct their abodes near deep water, and that reason alone makes these structures potential spring through fall hot spots. Texas-rigged plastic worms and weighted nymphs are solid choices during the spring and fall but go topwater during the summer.

Brush Piles

Brush piles can occur anywhere at any time on a body of water. However, they are most likely to come into being during the spring when debris washes down river and accumulates in certain locales. The most productive brush piles almost always lie on outside bends where, by definition, deeper water exists. And the best piles there will be those that lie under several feet of water and are thus less visible to anglers. On summer days when shadows extend across this cover, running a topwater across brush can be quite worthwhile. Any other time, cast nymph and crayfish patterns and jig and pigs and plastic concoctions.

Stickups

Stickups are ideal forms of cover to apply the run-and-gun gambit to, regardless of the season. Isolated stickups are too easy to spot and work, so I prefer stickups in a group, especially if deeper water is nearby. From several different angles, run a spinnerbait or minnow pattern through these fields and then move on. Anglers pound thin water stickups throughout the year, but those in shallow environs rarely hold fish after the spawn. Both human-made and natural wood can draw smallmouth bass throughout much of the year. Develop patterns for fishing this cover on your home body of water, and you will likely experience more success.

Chapter 28

Return to Yesteryear:
Going after America's Small Stream Bass

I have a confession to make. I am 55 years old, and I am still fishing some of the small streams that I journeyed to as a boy—when my most prized fishing possessions (make that most prized possessions of any kind) were a worn-out spincaster; a cheap, two-piece fiberglass rod; and purple, silver, and gold Rebel minnows. One summer on a beautiful July morning, a friend and I went wade fishing on an isolated mountain smallmouth creek that I had first visited as a youngster, even though I could have joined other buddies at a major impoundment that was much closer to my home.

In five hours of fishing, my cohort and I dueled with nearly a dozen small stream smallies with one of the fish easily topping three pounds. Meanwhile, on the nearby bass lake, one of my friends boated a 12-inch largemouth, the only "keeper" that his party managed to catch. What's more, my friend seemed quite pleased with his performance; he later went into great detail explaining how, "given the conditions" (warm water, indifferent bass, and boating and fishing pressure), he had enjoyed an extremely satisfactory outing.

I have no desire to take away my friend's fishing self-esteem, and I enjoy lake fishing for black bass as much as anyone. But here is a basic fishing fact that, in this era of major impoundments, high performance bass boats, and high stakes angling, definitely needs to be emphasized. Across America, this country's small streams boast thriving populations of either largemouth, smallmouth, or spotted bass—depending on the region of the country and the physical conditions (such as water temperature and flow) of the creeks themselves. What's more, these streams can be as different as upland smallmouth rills in the Northeast and Southeast, inner city or lowland largemouth creeks in the heartland and on both coasts, and spotted bass streams in the hill country of the South.

Two other basic fishing facts also need to be emphasized. The major reason why such high quality bassing for largemouths, smallies, and spots exists in these mini-waterways is because of the Clean Water Act from the 1960s. Before that time, many of these streams, especially in urban areas, were badly polluted. Whenever I hear businesses or individuals rail against "big government" not letting them do what they want (and what too many companies want is to more freely pollute the nation's air and water), I like to remind them of the Clean Water Act and the establishment of our treasured national forests as being "big government" actions that have been so important to outdoorsmen. (Obviously, not all big government or "big business" policies have been beneficial to sportsmen.)

And, second, because of the glamour of lake fishing, these small streams are extremely under fished. I have gained permission to wade fish streams in rural, mountain areas, well-developed suburbs, and in heavily populated cities. Indeed, I have rarely been refused access in a lifetime of angling. I am convinced that the black bass in many of these little waterways rarely see a lure or fly—and their aggressive nature often seems to indicate such. A polite request issued to a landowner should result in your access to the small stream nearest you.

How to Fish Small Streams

Small stream success begins with developing an understanding of why being able to quietly wade upstream is crucial. Like current-dwelling fish anywhere, stream bass position themselves facing upstream so that they can engulf minnows, crayfish, and various aquatic and terrestrial species that drift downstream. By wading into the current, you are much less likely to be seen by the bass.

But the fish will definitely detect your presence if you do not approach silently, taking great care to gently slide your feet over the bottom. Anglers should imitate how great blue herons and other members of the heron and crane families hunt for aquatic prey. These predators remain motionless for long periods of time, only moving with a purpose and only then for short distances in a stealthy manner.

Lure and fly presentation is similarly crucial. Dale Huggins, an expert fly fisherman from Richmond, Virginia, maintains that small stream bass suggest to him a certain salmonid.

Don't Downsize Your Baits and Flies for Small Stream Bass

I don't like to downsize my flies and soft plastic baits when I fish mini-waterways. The unfortunate result is often that too many pint-sized bass and sunfish will hit my offerings. Instead, I tie on the same size 2 and 4 poppers and 6-inch worms and lizards and 4-inch craw worms and ringworms that I normally use and either fish the soft plastics sans weights or with a split shot or two crimped 12 or so inches above the bait. For example, the 5-pound smallmouth that I mentioned earlier fell to a weightless ringworm. My favorite bait to split shot, though, is a craw worm which, when rigged in this manner and hopped across the substrate, very accurately mimics the actions of the real thing.

"Creek bass remind me a great deal of brown trout," said Huggins. "Both are ambush feeders, and both look for places where they don't have to fight the current. Both also react negatively to any unnatural noises in their environments. The only difference between the two is that brown trout are more of a low light feeder than creek bass are. Successful fishermen, whether they use fly or spinning rods, will have to be able to make long, accurate casts."

For long rodders, Huggins recommends 7- to 8-foot, 3- to 4-weight rods. Since most creeks are very narrow, and because the best ones are often choked with streamside growth, longer rods are definitely not an option. For casting distance and accuracy with a spinning outfit, I prefer a 6-foot medium or medium action rod, spooled with 8-pound test.

Now some readers will no doubt question why I opt for such relatively heavy line, since most small streams have very clear, shallow water with depths generally under eight feet and often much less than that. My biggest small stream bass was a smallmouth that weighed over five pounds and that was finning about in a 2-foot pool in a creek that

Want to experience some quality small stream smallmouth action? Return to yesteryear and wade fish a creek near you.

was just 18 feet wide. If I had not had 8-pound test in that situation, I have no doubt that the brute would have broken the line.

Make no mistake—because America's small streams are so under fished, some truly nice-sized bass dwell in them. Don't expect to catch the next world record largemouth, smallmouth, or spot, though. But don't be surprised if your local creek holds numerous bass that top two and three pounds.

Lures and Flies to Consider

When creek fishing, the challenge is to employ larger lures and patterns that attract bigger bass but at the same time won't alarm bass in the clear, shallow water characteristic of many mini-waterways. For example, although spinnerbaits and crankbaits perform excellently as lake bass lures, they are often quite ineffective on small streams. Spinnerbaits especially create too much disturbance when they land, and crankbaits often create too much water displacement when retrieved. If you downsize these two baits in the form of inline spinners and ultralight cranks, then you will mostly attract panfish and smaller bass. Additionally, sink tip lines and weighted patterns have little practical use on creeks and their typically shallow water environs.

The solution, then, is to use lures and flies that mimic creatures naturally found in the environment. For instance, when I was a boy, I collected salamanders from springs and branches. The bass in the creek near my home eagerly pounced on these creatures. I can still remember the thrill of a smallmouth swimming up to a salamander struggling across the surface, and then watching the fish tear off with the creature as my line played out and my excitement rose. Today, 4- to 6-inch plastic lizards are among my favorite creek lures.

Other deadly creek flies and lures are a crayfish pattern and a 4-inch craw worm, and the reason for my preference for them likewise lies in my childhood. A chum and I liked to visit a creek that featured a limestone pool that was fairly deep (about six feet) for a stream, but unusually narrow (only about four feet wide). We had often seen 3-pound plus bronzebacks finning about, but we could never maneuver close enough, given the streamside vegetation, to fire off an accurate cast.

One day after unsuccessfully angling for the fish for well over an hour, I turned away from the pool and walked about 20 yards upstream. Taking off my baseball-style cap and using it as a seine, I managed to corral a rather large crawdad. Ten minutes later, I had landed a previously uncatchable jumbo creek smallie. Soft plastic crawdads rigged Texas-style or with a split shot (see accompanying sidebar) have similar effects on bass today as do Clouser Crayfish.

Regarding locales to fish, a number stand out as prime small stream hot spots. Dale Huggins lists eddies, rock piles, undercut banks, and underwater obstructions such as logjams, fallen trees, and brush piles. Beaver dams are common on many streams that I wade fish, and the downstream sides of aquatic vegetation where the water is typically deeper can also host black bass.

Great Fly Patterns for Small Streams

Dale Huggins lists several patterns that have produced well for him on small streams. A great year-round choice is a No. 8 or 10 Woolly Bugger. For cold water conditions, the long rodder weights it with dumb bell eyes. For warm water action, Huggins suggests hair bugs in a host of patterns.

"Creek bass seem to like the way a hair bug feels in their mouths, as opposed to hard poppers which they seem to reject too quickly," he said.

And for jumbo stream bass, which he defines as any over 15 inches, Huggins relies on size 2 Dahlberg Divers. These are especially effective in low light conditions.

Plying Small Streams Can Make You a Better Lake and River Angler

If fishing for unpressured bass in underutilized streams is not enough to make you a dedicated creek angler, then consider this. The knowledge you gain from plying small stream bass can make you a much better river, lake, or reservoir fisherman. For example, actually observing how bass hold in creeks can help you understand, and more importantly visualize, how bass locate in power generation lakes. These black bass face into the current and situate themselves in many of the same types of places as their small stream counterparts do.

Plus, if you can learn how to accurately cast in the cramped confines of a mini-waterway, then you will likely have little difficulty making accurate presentations to bass that hold in out-of-the way locations, such as under docks and beneath overhanging trees. And if you have ever had a nice bass spook at your approach because you dragged instead of slid your feet against the bottom, then you have a real idea of how lake bass can become alarmed at any of the sounds that emanate from a bass boat, such as a trolling motor being engaged or a tackle box being dropped.

In the long ago days of the early 1900s, many if not most American anglers actually depended on excursions to small streams for both food and fun. Today, the American angling public seems to regard these waterways with sort of a benign neglect. Hopefully more anglers will come to regard the country's small streams as the natural treasures that they are.